If you've ever felt like you were going to
THROW UP, FREEZE UP or PASS OUT . . .

HOW TO AVOID EMBARRASSMENT & HUMILIATION IN PUBLIC SPEAKING

"I have never been able to pin point my fears and this book nailed it with every paragraph!"

Trish U.

"Loved it! Leah is so relatable because she hasn't always been comfortable in front of crowds and that inspires those of us who struggle with public speaking."

Mary Beth J.

HOW TO AVOID EMBARRASSMENT & HUMILIATION IN PUBLIC SPEAKING

Leah Hoppes

FIRST EDITION

KINGMAN ROW
Johnston, IA

HOW TO AVOID EMBARRASSMENT & HUMILIATION IN PUBLIC SPEAKING. Copyright ©2017 by Leah Hoppes. All rights reserved. Manufactured in the United States of America. No part of this book may be reproduced in any form or by any means (whether mechanical or electronic, including information storage and retrieval systems) without the express written permission of the publisher. Exception shall be made for reviewers or other profilers of the book or the author, who may quote passages of up to 300 words.

Published by Kingman Row Entertainment, LLC, 5874 Merle Hay Road, Unit 1159, Johnston, IA 50131 (515) 321-1507.

First edition.
For more information about Kingman Row Entertainment, LLC, visit www.kingmanrowentertainment.com

For more information about Leah Hoppes, visit www.leahhoppes.com

Publisher's Cataloging-In-Publication Data
(Prepared by The Donohue Group, Inc.)

Name: Hoppes, Leah.
Title: How To Avoid Embarrassment & Humiliation in Public Speaking / Leah Hoppes
Description: First edition. | Johnston, IA: Kingman Row Entertainment, [2017] | Series: [Chomp series] | Summary: "If you've ever felt like you were going to throw up, freeze up, or pass out, this books is for you! Public Speaking doesn't need to be intimidating and it can be mastered with the right tools." – Provided by publisher.
Identifiers: LCCN 2017951879 | ISBN 978-0-9960746-6-7 | ISBN 0-9960746-6-X
Subjects: LCSH: Public speaking—psychological aspects. | Hoppes, Leah.
Classification: LCC PN4129.15.H66 2017 | DDC 808.51—dc23

Leah Hoppes. 1st edition.

Author photograph by Alex Claney Photography

Edited by James Serpento

Dedicated to my mother

CONTENTS

Acknowledgments		9
Preface		11
Chapter 1	The Great Survey	17
Chapter 2	Stars Not Born That Way	23
Chapter 3	Love it, Hate it or Meh	30
Chapter 4	It's the Teacher's Fault	34
Chapter 5	No Need for Speed	39
Chapter 6	Control It	43
Chapter 7	E-Nun-See-Ate	48
Chapter 8	Your Better Voice	62
Chapter 9	Easy as Conversation	70
Chapter 10	Creating the Text	73
Chapter 11	Content with Integrity	81
Chapter 12	Avoid the Crutch	86
Chapter 13	Perfect Practice	93
Chapter 14	Check Your Props	104
Chapter 15	Let's Get Physical	108
Chapter 16	Own Your Room	119
Chapter 17	Edifying	125

Chapter 18	The Big Day	132
Chapter 19	When Murphy Speaks	136
Chapter 20	Next Steps	146
Chapter 21	Warm Up Exercises	150

Acknowledgments

This book is possible because of my mother's strength which has been the foundation for my life. I have tried to mirror her grace under pressure, to remain strong in front of those who preferred me weaker, and to hold steadfast where others have waivered. It is because of her strength of spirit, passed on to me, that I have been able to take giants leaps of faith.

Heartfelt thanks to Trish Urzedowski who asked a question which spurred me to finish this book, four years after I had created the initial manuscript. It was the kick in the pants I needed!

A very big thank you to Marjorie Stradinger, Mary Beth Jones, Christine Flood and Tracy Minnec for taking the time to provide valuable feedback on early stages of the manuscript.

Huge thank you to James Serpento and Tom Laspisa for the thankless job of editing my work.

Thank you to Milos Subotic for the Chomp™ artwork and Arnolfo Santoro for the cover design.

And, of course, thank you to my husband, Sean Matthew Whitfield for his unconditional love and support.

Preface

"We don't rise to the level of our expectations, we fall to the level of our training."

— Archilochos

Public Speaking is one of those subjects that elicits a strong reaction from many people. Whether it's fear of being judged, nervousness about what to say, or simply hating the idea of being uncomfortable, public speaking causes a lot of anxiety.

After years of public speaking and coaching people to be better presenters, I've uncovered a few common themes that keep individuals from being their best. It really boils down to practice and preparation.

I've heard that the United States Marine Corps, uses a variation on Archilochos's quote: *"You will not rise to the occasion, you will sink to the level of your preparation."*

When I first heard that, my reaction was "Yes! That's exactly how it is with public speaking!" Inexperienced speakers believe they will figure it out, or "rise to the occasion" when in fact, they inevitably "sink to the level of their preparation."

What keeps you from being a more confident and polished speaker is *better preparation!*

Do you need this book? You tell me.

Have you ever felt like you weren't meant to speak in front of people? Perhaps you've gone your whole life thinking that public speaking was only reserved for other people.

If that's the case, this book is for you.

Maybe you've been embarrassed by that flash of heat rising in your cheeks while speaking or have been totally demoralized by your public speaking skills.

You need this book.

Have you ever been so frustrated and disappointed in how you spoke that you kicked yourself for days?

You will learn from this book.

Perhaps you have been so humiliated by your performance that you cried afterward? It happens to more people than you know!

Maybe you've experienced dry mouth and clammy hands, or have stuttered and sweated your way through enough presentations that, now, you just avoid anything that resembles public speaking.

This book will help you.

"Wait a minute, I'm already a good speaker!" you might be saying.

Great! I've got tools for you too!

Of course, there's also the possibility that you've never really done any public speaking, but something has prompted you to pick up this book.

This won't disappoint.

So, if you've ever felt like you were going to THROW UP, FREEZE UP, or PASS OUT at the thought of public speaking . . . you've got the right book!

If you simply just want to be more poised and polished in front of an audience . . . this book is for you.

Why am I so confident that I can help? Because not only did I overcome a childhood speech impediment, I've been speaking in front of people since competing on my high school speech team.

I didn't just learn how to speak, I also learned how to do so in all types of venues. One school was so limited on space that I literally had to give a presentation in a broom closet, complete with mops and buckets. From closets to auditoriums, I learned how to command attention and own my room.

That early experience led to opportunities to speak publicly in front of large groups in other venues and then I went on to study theatre in college where I began to conquer stage performance. By the time I graduated college, I had spoken in front of people around 1,000 times.

After school, I entered corporate America where I had roles which required presenting to peers and to C level executives. I was even asked to co-facilitate corporate training leadership classes alongside the full-time trainers.

Now, as business owners, my husband and I hold workshops and seminars and lead corporate training on subjects like marketing, sales, leadership, entrepreneurship – and public speaking.

All of this experience has trained me in not only *how to speak* but also *how to prepare* for public speaking opportunities.

Throughout my career, I've found myself coming back time and time again to the very same principles I learned during speech competition. I give the credit for my success to my mother and speech coach, Rhea Hoppes. A talent in her own right, she has achieved the National Speech and Debate Association (formerly National Forensic League) Three Diamond level. Her belief that "to be great, one must practice at being great" is a philosophy that I've continued to live by.

By combining my mom's expert knowledge, wisdom and compassion with my own 30 years of experience in speaking and coaching, I've developed tools which demystify the term "public speaker" as an elusive, elitist category.

So, let's dive into how you can avoid any future embarrassment and humiliation in public speaking!

1

THE GREAT SURVEY

We are fed all sorts of nonsense from the time we're little, and even though most of it isn't done with malicious intent, the myths and misinformation can give us excuses to avoid doing things we are perfectly capable of doing.

You've probably heard a variation on one of the following statements: "Public speaking is the biggest fear, second only to death," or, "People are more afraid of public speaking than they are of death."

Like you, I've heard this over and over again and I was curious about where this originated. I started researching the source of this fear of public speaking statement and found out something I wasn't expecting.

In 1973 R.H. Bruskin & Associates[1] took a survey of 2,543 adult men and women. The survey was comprised of a list of things or situations one might fear such as speaking before a group, deep water, heights, etc. The result showed that 40.6% listed speaking in front of a group higher than the fear of heights which came in at 32% while death came in lower on the list with only 18% of the vote.

Public speaking did, in fact, rank higher as a fear than the fear of death. That certainly makes for great headlines, but it's important to understand that the respondents weren't ever asked what their biggest fear was, nor were they asked to rank their fears. The survey results were based on the fear that was selected *the most*. So, actually, we don't know what those participants' primary fear was, we only know the most common fear among them was the fear of public speaking.

In the past 40 years since that survey, speculation has been cast on those results. Allegedly, Bruskin used such reports for promotional purposes. A more recent survey of 1,016 college students indicated that fear of snakes came in higher than the fear of speaking in front of a group. This time, fear of death outranked the fear of public speaking.

Does this mean adults develop a greater fear of speaking in front of groups at a certain age? Since the studies were conducted 40 years apart maybe it was a generational shift? We simply don't know.

I took a post-graduate statistics class and the first thing the professor said was, "The first rule of statistics: never trust statistics." He then proceeded to show us in study after study how the results of the same research could be used to support opposing views based on how the data was presented.

As I read about these two studies, I could see how the data was taken out of context. The first one is marred by a weak line of questioning. The second survey sampled fewer people who were actually enrolled in a communications course. Would an individual who really feared public speaking enroll in a class where it might be part of the curriculum? Could that skew the results? I think it's entirely possible.

This whole "public speaking is the number-one fear" has been miscommunicated and therefore overblown. A common fear, yes – both studies appear to support that. But some of you have heard about this fear of public speaking and have internalized it. You may have used it as an excuse not to do something you want or need to do.

Even if public speaking is a real fear for you, it may not be as big a fear as you've made it out to be. Or, if it is a very big fear for you, perhaps it will dissipate by reading where your fear comes from and provide some freedom of thought by showing you that you really can overcome it.

When I ask clients where they fall on the spectrum of loving versus hating public speaking, most people will tell me, "I don't *hate* it . . ." and I can literally see some of their tension disperse. Simply acknowledging that it isn't as big as they had made it out to be gives them more personal power over it.

Once we stop calling it a fear and simply start addressing it as what it really is – a skill that needs to be improved – all of a sudden the goal of being a better public speaker becomes more attainable. From a psychological standpoint, it no longer has as tight of a grip on our psyche.

I'd go as far as to say that there are other things you would more actively avoid than public speaking but you just don't think about them as frequently. Take a minute to read the following and really be honest with yourself.

Would you rather give up the roof over your head and allow the bank to take your home away (and no, you wouldn't be absolved of your mortgage payment) or do you think you could possibly muster the courage to speak for a couple of minutes in front of your peers at work?

Most of you would be able to mumble a few words despite the queasiness if being homeless were a very real alternative.

Let's lessen the severity: how about you wire transfer $1,000 cash to me right now, or you figure out a way to chatter on about something for three minutes in front of a group.

I would wager that most of you would put up with butterflies or sweaty palms in order to avoid handing over that much money without receiving anything in return.

Some of you aren't really afraid of the spotlight, you're afraid of being judged by the audience. You might not fear to be in front of people but are unsure of how to handle yourself in situations where you have to control a room. Many forms of insecurity typically get rolled up into "fear of public speaking."

Have you been using any of those fears as an excuse to keep you from speaking in front of people? Has that fear kept you from jobs that would require you to speak in front of a group?

Don't give up on yourself! I believe every single person who tells me they don't like public speaking has untapped potential to be a good (if not great!) speaker.

2

STARS NOT BORN THAT WAY

Being a great public speaker doesn't mean you were born with something special. It just means you have mastered certain techniques.

Now, there is more to being a great speaker than some would lead you to believe, but it's also less complicated than others make it out to be.

Some will tell that in order to be a great speaker all you have to do is "practice more." The problem with *that* is that, if you're practicing the *wrong* way, you're not going to get better. This would be like telling you to practice a bad golf swing a thousand times. Practicing wrong does not make you better. It makes you *worse!*

Not even practicing the right way is foolproof. If you're inclined to talk too fast, too slow or in a monotone, no matter how much "right practice" you have, you're still going to be hard to listen to. But, more on that later. Right now, we're going to explore some of the barriers you might have had with public speaking.

Made Not Born

Being the center of attention doesn't come naturally for everyone. Many people initially recoil from the thought of having all eyes on them or having to speak in front of a group of people. Sometimes it is only through maturity or necessity that individuals become comfortable speaking in front of groups.

It's easy to forget this when we see a comedian on TV and hear he's been making people laugh since he was five. Then there's the singer who says she's been singing since she was three. We'll hear a dancer's mom claim her daughter started dancing in the crib. OK, I made that last one up, but really, doesn't it feel like everybody had an earlier start than we did?

Sure, these anecdotes are cute, but what message does that send to the already discouraged masses?

It's easy to fall into a trap of thinking that because, a long time ago, we choked in front of a crowd, that we're not meant to do public speaking. Too many people have bought into the lie that "I'm not good in front of people."

Just because we didn't come out of the womb confident and articulate doesn't mean we can't learn to be so.

Allow me to extend hope because:

I believe everyone has the ability to improve their public speaking and presentation skills with the right techniques.

"Yeah, easy for you to say," you might be thinking to yourself. But, before you make a snap judgment, take a step back in time with me . . . .

At the age of six, my mom took me to enroll in ballet class, but I refused. I don't even know why I was so adamant against signing up for classes. I loved watching my sister in the dance studio and I imitated the barre exercises while she was in class. At home, I would even put on her ballet shoes and dance around in them.

Not only did I love ballet, I loved all things pink! All four walls of my room were painted bright pink. One would be crazy to think I would turn down the opportunity to put on pink tights, a pink leotard and to wear soft pink shoes.

Either I lacked the imagination to see myself actually dancing, or maybe I was just demonstrating the Hoppes family trait of stubbornness. All I can tell you for sure is that I wasn't scared, I just didn't have the wherewithal to conceive of myself doing it.

An early experience of limited thinking to be sure. Oh, but my self-limiting beliefs did not stop there!

One year later, at the ripe ol' age of seven, I was finally ready to take classes. After several months, my dance teacher announced that she would be auditioning for a lead in the spring recital. We were to audition during our regular class time. No adults or outsiders were around, just my classmates.

I was the only one who wouldn't audition.

I remember sitting there cross-legged with my back against the mirror watching as the rest of my classmates, twirled, swirled and sashayed across the studio. Everyone kept coaxing me, urging and encouraging me - but I wouldn't, or maybe I couldn't, budge.

All I had to do was a simple run, run, leeeaap across the floor, which was something I loved to do! But under pressure, with all the eyes on me, I refused.

Several months later, my dance teacher told my older sister that she had wanted to give me the role, all I had to do was audition.

The only thing I had to do was what I had done every other week in class: do what the rest of my classmates were doing, and I would've been selected for the starring role.

My teacher had identified something special about me, but she couldn't just hand the role over to me. She needed me to audition – but I didn't. I tied her hands because she couldn't award me something that I didn't even try to win.

How often do we miss opportunities because of fear or self-consciousness or, as in my case, a simple refusal to participate?

Here's the myth I'm trying to bust in sharing all of this with you. Not all performers are "born that way," and certainly not all great speakers have been speaking eloquently since they were six.

My early years were full of being timid and reserved and it took me a long time to be able to get outside of myself. That early experience of missing out has served as a valuable life lesson in what I could miss out on if I choose not to participate.

Not everyone you see performing who appears to be a "natural" was always such a natural. Many of us continued to work at it and have had to overcome things like shyness and speech impediments. We've had to practice and practice and practice *and practice* until we got it right. By doing it more than everyone else, we became better than everyone else.

Did I win every single speech meet, win every role I auditioned for, and ace every presentation? Absolutely not. In fact, I've had my share of being embarrassed and feeling humiliated by my lack of preparation in front of audiences. But every horrible experience made me want to be better. Sometimes it really just comes down to doing something longer and wanting something more than the next person. That resolve means a willingness to do what others aren't willing to do.

What does this mean for you?

It means that if you've bought into the lie that you were born "without the performance gene" or you've fed yourself the baloney that you "can't talk in front of people," I'm here to challenge you.

If a shy kid who couldn't say the word "third" or "roar" without being teased can go on to win speech competitions, speak in front of groups numbering in the thousands while still in high school, give business presentations on marketing strategy and product lines, impress C level executives, and then actually get paid as a public speaker, and public speaking coach, well then, my friend, *you* too can learn to be a better speaker.

Now, let's see which category of speaker you fall into.

3

LOVE IT, HATE IT or MEH

There are three types of people – those who love public speaking, those who hate public speaking, and most common of all, those who don't really hate it but actively avoid it.

Although a foreign concept for many, there are a whole lot of you who get really excited about speaking. You lose sleep, but it's because you're so busy preparing the perfect joke or crafting the pithy phrase. You're simply thrilled to get the chance to speak.

If this is you, hooray! Find more places to speak and the more you do it, the better you'll become.

But what if you're at the other end of the spectrum?

Say you are one of those who absolutely shuns speaking publicly at all costs. Then, sure enough, there's an occasion in which you find yourself forced to speak – as in, your job will be impacted. That speaking event probably makes you so nervous you would rather have a tooth pulled.

The mere thought of getting up in front of a group, (much less your peers), causes you stress, anxiety, sleepless nights, clammy hands, and in some cases, even nausea.

If you absolutely despise getting up in front of people, maybe you've realized, as one of my clients did, that fear of public speaking was the only thing keeping her from reaching her full business and revenue-making potential. Like her, you have decided you finally need to address this beast of a fear.

If this is where you fall on the spectrum, I hope you find that the following techniques provide you the lures to cage that fear and tame it, once and for all.

It has been my experience that the majority of you fall somewhere in between. You may not exactly detest speaking in front of people, but you've become pretty adept at *not* volunteering for any position which would require you to stand up in front of a group and talk. When you have been suckered into anything that resembles a presentation, you're the one who talks from your seat, allowing the emphasis to be on someone else or your slides. You pretend you're being informal just so you don't have to stand up. I'm hitting home with a few of you – I know it – because I've seen you in action.

If this is what you have endured for uncountable years, let me offer you some solace: you aren't odd, you aren't flawed, and many of you don't lack confidence in other areas. So what exactly is going on?

It's conditioning. Pure and simple.

Because I find the subject captivating, I started digging into it a bit and discovered something fascinating.

One group becomes **nervous**[2] (*adjective* 1. highly excitable; unnaturally or acutely uneasy or apprehensive: *to become nervous under* **stress**.*)*

A second group becomes **excited**[3] (*adjective* 1. stirred emotionally; agitated: *An excited crowd awaited the arrival of the famed rock group.*)

The definition of the word nervous is highly *excitable*. Isn't it interesting that the very definition of "nervous" is a form of the word "excite?"

Digging further, the word "excited" contains "agitated" in the definition. The word "agitated" can mean "excited" or . . . "disturbed."

So you see, it's possible to interpret (i.e. become "nervous" about) something– say, *the thought of public speaking* – in either a positive or negative way!

What makes the difference? Choice? Genetics? Whether or not there's an R in the month?

Just *why* do so many people *hate* talking in front of other people?

4

IT'S THE TEACHER'S FAULT

Many of us were introduced to public speaking in the most barbaric of modern-day circumstances – middle school English class.

Whoever decided this was a good idea, clearly, was never a kid. Middle school happens at a point in our lives when we are the most socially, physically and emotionally compromised, and certainly vulnerable to peer pressure.

I tend to believe whichever teacher came up with this torturous notion either hated humanity or simply had a great many self-loathing issues. Either way, he or she effectively raised up generations who avoid speaking in front of others.

Are you beginning to understand that it isn't that you are a bad speaker, or that you are in any way inferior to peers who enjoy public speaking? More likely, you were the victim of some ruthless teacher whose idea of fun was to make you stand up and talk on a topic you knew nothing about – and then grade you on it! To make matters even worse, you had to speak in front of the same kids who got their kicks making fun of your nose or your choice of jeans.

See where some of your anxiety might stem from?

We would have all been better off had the idea of show 'n tell grown up with us, rather than being left behind in grade school. If it had transitioned with us as we matured then we might have learned how to speak in front of any presenter's toughest audience, our peers, without any qualms. That would have led to being able to speak comfortably in front of any type of crowd.

Had we continued learning how to present on subjects we knew very well, we would have had a greater chance to develop confidence. With the consistent experience of talking confidently, we could have become more comfortable presenting product line gaps within our market, or our sales territory numbers. Yes, talking about our favorite doll, our doggy, or our Darth Vader action figure would still be distant memories, but the value of learning how to speak passionately about something would have overridden our fear.

Over the past thirty-some years, I've discovered there is one primary element which separates a good speaker from a bad one: the presence – or lack of – nervousness.

Bad speeches and horrible presentations are most commonly a result of the speaker's nervousness. What causes those nerves? It happens when we aren't focused on the subject, but rather, are focused on ourselves, or what others might think of us.

Once we've shifted the focus from ourselves to the subject we are sharing, we instantly become better presenters. When we learn how to focus solely on the material and become passionate about teaching the audience, then the agitation is no longer *nervousness*. Rather, it transforms into *excitement*.

I'm referring to more than just confidence. Certainly being confident in your subject matter is key, but I haven't found that a general lack of confidence is the source of the problem with public speakers. These individuals are usually very confident in all other areas of their personal or professional lives.

Furthermore, all of my clients have been confident in their material. The issue is that they *lack confidence in their skills to speak in front of people*. That's primarily because they are focusing on the wrong things and not utilizing the right tools.

Stop allowing the little voice in your head to tell you that you're not good in front of a crowd, and start thinking about public speaking more as show 'n tell, a simple sharing of your thoughts.

Why?

Well, first, if you think of speaking in front of a room as being as easy as show 'n tell – which you likely remember as that delicious opportunity to *share* – you'll likely find the whole thing less intimidating.

Second – and most important – *you have experience!*

If you could do something as a kid, don't you think you can certainly do it now? You remember how. You did it 20, 30, 45 years ago, and just like riding a bike, once your brain and body have collaborated, they know they can do it again. Sure there might be a bit of swerving when you hop on wheels for the first time in a couple of decades, but you know how to do it because you have done it.

I hear you now. "Yes, but I hated show 'n tell!" Really? You hated hugging your stuffed bear and telling people his name? Weren't you happy to have the excuse to bring him to school?

I gotta tell you, I have yet to meet a kid who doesn't overflow with newly and easily minted words about that stuffed bear, or the video game they've just mastered, or virtually any other part of their world, all while effortlessly making their visual aids available.

What if you are one of those who really didn't like show 'n tell? I cannot hope to address every single human experience here, but I do hope that you will continue reading because I have some tips which will help you.

Let's explore them!

5

NO NEED FOR SPEED

Whether it's because they just have so much to say or their nerves get the better of them, some presenters start talking fast and gain momentum, leaving audiences exhausted.

Perhaps you've been in the audience and may not have been aware of why you didn't "feel" like you got a particular message. Maybe you thought you weren't really focused or you felt a little drained afterward.

You may not have realized it, but the likelihood is that the presenter was simply speaking so fast that just trying to listen wore you out. His speech pattern was so rapid that you didn't hear every word and your brain was then forced to fill in the blanks. The result was that you left not really understanding what you heard.

The speaker will walk away wondering why no one even bothered to ask a question or won't understand why he didn't connect.

Think of radio or TV ads where the disclaimer is spoken in a rapid-fire voiceover. You may have gotten the gist – that the company is absolved of any and all responsibility – but you certainly didn't hear every word, and let's face it, you didn't really care, did you? Did you ever play this back because you were dying to hear the details? No, because you couldn't focus on it and therefore you assumed it was irrelevant, nothing more than the obligatory addition to a commercial.

What'sitliketoreadthisandhowdoesitmakeyoufeelandwouldyoureadawholebookwrittenthisway?

For the same reason that there are spaces in written language, so should there be spaces – pauses, silences, hesitations – when speaking. Experienced speakers know how to pause for dramatic effect, or to stop to engage their audience in a question, but a less experienced and otherwise solid speaker can lose a great deal of influence when they rush through their presentation.

The object of public speaking is to communicate to the audience and these "spaces" give us the breathing room for understanding.

When we hear a rushed speaker, two things happen to us as listeners. First, we miss words and we insert what we think was said. Second, we get tired and we stop trying to listen. When that happens we only absorb a fraction of what's being communicated. Both events are disastrous for a speaker because it means you're losing your audience!

I've seen otherwise very seasoned public speakers make this mistake. It's something you expect from an overzealous teenager, but in the professional world, we are positioning ourselves as an expert in a certain area. Not being in control of your speaking pattern comes across as immature, unsure of yourself, or even that you're hopped up on caffeine. All of which undermine your authority.

Slow Down.

Slowing the tempo can make the difference between an average speaker and a polished presenter.
But wait! We can't end the chapter here because it's also possible to have an opposite problem.

I attended an alleged "professional speakers group" where they're supposed to train people how to be better speakers and yet the speakers talked so slowly that it was painful to listen to. Speaking. Like. A. Robot. Is. Not. Better.

Hard to read? Harder still to listen to! It can actually be worse than talking too fast because now we all know you're self-conscious, and it can sound like you're "dumbing down" your presentation.

Yes, you need to articulate and yes, you need to slow down if your natural tendency is to speak too fast, but don't do anything that feels artificial, because that's exactly how it will come across.

It's common sense – that's all it really is. You want to speak at your natural pace but with a healthy, varied jaunt to keep things dynamic.

Be natural, be you, in all your aliveness. Be you – just improved.

6

CONTROL IT

Have you ever left your cell phone upstairs and then madly rushed up, two stairs at a time, to pick up an important phone call? Pretending to be calm, you started talking to help stop the heavy breathing. If you've done this while being really out-of-breath you've felt your chest tighten at the restriction of air flow. Did you notice how you sounded? Your voice was likely tighter and a bit higher than usual.

Let's try something: Take a deep breath in and then exhale.

Did your shoulders raise up and your chest expand? Or, did you feel your lower belly expand out?

Unless you're a singer, actor or yoga enthusiast, you probably were in the first group. Most people don't practice deep breathing. If you have had musical training, practiced yoga, or Pilates, you were probably in the group who felt your belly button expand. This is ideal for public speaking because this is how you begin to control your breath.

When we take our breath all the way in so that it expands and contracts our diaphragm, we have just gained more control over our breath because the lungs themselves are not muscles; it's the diaphragm that is the muscle which controls our breathing.

If we inhale and the air settles in our chest without engaging the diaphragm fully, we won't have the same degree of control over our breath. Our breathing will be shallow and more rapid.

When, and how, you inhale and exhale will actually impact your vocal quality. This is why you need breath control.

Breathiness can weaken an otherwise great presentation because it exposes an inexperienced or very nervous speaker. Conversely, once you have learned to control your breath, you can be nervous and no one will ever know! You can actually calm yourself down simply by taking a few deep breaths to recalibrate your intake of air. Getting your breath under control will typically calm the rest of your nervous system too.

You do have control over your breathing and you can use your voice like any other tool.

Let's try an exercise that will help you practice breath control. When you first start this, you will likely not get very far, but keep practicing. This will help you control your breath in stressful situations. It will ultimately make you a better presenter because when you master breath control you start becoming a master of your voice.

I wrote the following exercise as I learned it back in college theatre. In researching the origins, I discovered a slightly different version that was used as a test for would-be radio announcers back in the 1920's.[4]

EXERCISE: Breath Control

This exercise is meant to help you learn how to control your breath and therefore your voice.

The idea here is to say as many of these phrases in one breath without sounding as if you're running out of breath. When you feel yourself starting to run out of breath, take another breath.

The primary purpose is to practice speaking while controlling when you take a breath. What I mean by that is, when you have control over your breath, you won't need to stop mid-sentence to take another breath. You will have conditioned yourself to take a breath at a natural break.

The ultimate goal, over time, is to recite this entire thing in one, controlled breath.

Ready? Go to the next page, get your breath under control and let's see how you do!

One Hen

Two ducks

Three squawking geese

Four Limerick oysters

Five corpulent porpoises

Six pairs of Don Alvero's tweezers

Seven thousand Macedonians in full battle array

Eight brass monkeys from the ancient sacred crypts of Egypt

Nine apathetic, diabetic, sympathetic old men on roller skates who have a marked propensity towards procrastination and sloth

Ten lyrical, spherical, diabolical, denizens of the deep who all stalk around the crack in the corner of the quarry at the same time

Whew! How far did you make it? Try it again and see if you can get further through the sequence.

7

E-NUN-SEE-ATE

In order to speak coherently and fluently you must **enunciate** – which means not only that you pronounce words correctly, but that you do so with crisp consonants and full, open vowels. Vowels carry the "melody" of speech; consonants – when they're clear and crisp – "drive" our speech, giving it momentum and energy.

Work at correcting lazy, slurred and sloppy speech patterns. Although this is how most people talk, it isn't ideal and it results in all sorts of misunderstandings.

If you're going to tell people to read the book titled "Ask" but what they hear is "Axe" or "Ass," well, you've got a problem. Enunciate!

Let's try something: read this number out loud: **20**

What did you say? Did you hear yourself say "twenny?" That's OK, many people will. Or, perhaps you fell into the minority of those who say "twe**nty**?"

I'm not picking on you if you were in the first group and I certainly don't want you to sound stilted, but I *am* trying to help you understand that if we're more careful and exact in our speech, our audience will have an easier time understanding us.

When the audience understands us, we're more effective in presenting our message.

The more precise we are in our speech, the better we will be at public speaking.

As you become more aware of your speech patterns and enunciation you may also become more aware of your regional accent. If English isn't your first language you may struggle with the pronunciation of certain words, and that's OK.

I don't want you to eliminate what makes you uniquely you, or become overly self-conscious.

I simply want you to be aware of how you sound to your audience so you can be the best presenter you can be.

What if you have a lisp, stutter, or type of speech impediment that you've been embarrassed about or that has kept you from being a confident speaker? Please, do not let that discourage you! You can either embrace it as part of who you are or you can hire a speech therapist who can help.

Remember, I had a speech impediment as a kid. I was one of those who would say "Next yeaww I'm going to be in thward gawade." I went through two years of speech therapy.

Sometimes these characteristics can add a richness and authenticity to you as a speaker, not to mention encourage others who have felt otherwise unqualified to speak in front of groups.

Bottom-line, you need to receive honest, objective feedback to determine if your concern is really keeping you from effectively communicating. If it is, then I would encourage you to seek out a speech therapist for an evaluation. Speech therapists and speech-language pathologists provide help with everything from pronunciation to stuttering to accent reduction.

If you're interested in learning more about how to use your voice and really improve your vocal quality, I recommend the Audible version of Roger Love's *Set Your Voice Free: How to Get the Singing or Speaking Voice You Want*. As a vocal coach, Roger shares the exercises and techniques he uses with his clients which mirrors the training I received.

No matter what path you take, I hope you will learn to like your voice and accept it as part of your unique identity.

Verbal Fillers

Before we move into the enunciation exercises that follow, we need to address one more important aspect of public speaking: verbal fillers.

Most of us use some type of filler while we search for our next thought or appropriate word. It's normal and pretty common in everyday conversation and using them occasionally isn't detrimental. However, if you use them too frequently when public speaking, they can be irritating to the audience and make you sound nervous, even a little amateurish.

EXERCISE:

Record yourself explaining your favorite hobby. Talk about what you do and go into some detail of why you do it. The point is to extemporaneously explain something where you have to think a little bit while talking. When you play it back, I want you to count how many times you used fillers: "um," "uh," "err," or "well." You may even discover a filler unique to you, if that's the case, you need to count those too!

How many did you count? Just a couple? Nice, but don't celebrate just yet. Go back and listen again, did you really hear all of them? We can become so accustomed to what we want to say, or think we say, that often, we don't hear what we *actually* say.

Was the count the same? Did you hear a couple more? Did you have one or two?

What if you found yourself saying "um" every other sentence? It's OK, you can correct this.

The solution is to train yourself in your everyday speech which will help eliminate it from your pattern of speaking. Over time, you will no longer use them in front of a room either. So, the next time you catch yourself saying "um" simply just stop talking and think. Pause while you search for that word instead.

There's another benefit from learning to pause: it will show you how you can tell stories more effectively. I know you've never done it, but I've caught myself saying things like, "it was February, or wait, no, um, was it January?" The reality was the person I was telling my story to didn't need to know what month it was, and paying attention to my verbal fillers trained me to stop fumbling for irrelevant details and get to the point.

Just like with any habit, it will take some time to change. But, once you have removed verbal fillers you will become a more polished presenter.

Now, let's move onto a few tools to get your mouth, lips, tongue, and brain moving and working in unison.

These exercises are also from my college theatre days. Some of them are tongue twisters, some of them are just weird and, despite research to source the origins, all I could find were random chat rooms where people talk about the myriad variations of what they heard as children. Regardless of their original purpose, I have found them to be very helpful in correcting lazy speech patterns, which most of us have.

The idea behind each of these exercises is to articulate each syllable fully.

In the first example, you won't just speed through it as you typically would in conversation, rather you will enunci**ate** and exagger**ate** some of the consonants (you caught the underlining and bold, right? Those aren't typos.)

By practicing out loud you may be using muscles in your face you didn't know you had. Let's have some fun! Ready? Let's go!

EXERCISE: 1

In normal conversation, most people would say this phrase without really articulating the "d's" in the words "red" "good" "blood" and "bad." If we were to write it how most people would say it, it would look something like this: "Releathr, yelloleathr, gooblood, bablood"

What you must do to make this effective is instead say, "re**d** leather, yell**ow** leather, goo**d** bloo**d,** ba**d** bloo**d**." I've bolded the parts which you need to especially enunciate. Repeat this several times. Out Loud. Remember, you're practicing *public* speaking.

Re**d** Leath**er**, Yell**ow** Leath**er**
Goo**d** Bloo**d**, Ba**d** Bloo**d**

Re**d** Leath**er**, Yell**ow** Leath**er**
Goo**d** Bloo**d**, Ba**d** Bloo**d**

Re**d** Leath**er**, Yell**ow** Leath**er**
Goo**d** Bloo**d**, Ba**d** Bloo**d**

EXERCISE: 2

Go slowly at first and be sure you're enunciating the consonants in bold print. You would never talk like this in real life, of course. The idea is that, in practicing this exaggeration, you will start to reprogram your mouth, lips, and tongue to effectively articulate. Like athletes who jump up and down in quick, small jumps to get their blood flowing – they don't hop while competing – it is strictly to warm up. You're doing these exercises to prepare you for speaking more clearly.

Wha**t to do to** die to**day**
A**t** a minute or two 'til **t**wo
A thing di**stinctly** har**d t**o say
But harder still **to do**
For they'll be a**t tattoo** a**t** a twe**nty** 'til **t**wo
A**t** a twe**nty** 'til **t**wo 'til two **t**oday
An**d** the dragon will come a**t** the bea**t** of the drum
A**t** a minute or two 'til **t**wo
A**t** a minute or two 'til **t**wo **to**day
A**t** a minute or two 'til **t**wo

EXERCISE: 3

This is an exercise which is especially good if you do any type of recorded presentations, webinars, videos, etc. When being overly conscientious with articulating, some speakers have a tendency (myself included) to pop their "t's." What I mean by that is, if you were speaking into a microphone and you said "tot," you would hear an ever-so-slight popping sound at the second "t."

Say it out loud – go ahead . . . "To**t**" Did you hear it?

Let's try it again, only *this time* pull the tip of your tongue slightly back so instead of it hitting your front teeth, the tip of your tongue stops and hits the roof of your mouth . . . "Tot"

Did you hear the difference? Did you *feel* the difference? It's a bit muted, more controlled and you won't hear that popping sound off of the last "t."

While you go through the following exercise, listen closely to how your "t's" sound.

A tutor who tu**tored** the flute
Trie**d to** tu**tor t**wo tutors **to** toot
Sai**d** the two **to** the tutor,
Is i**t** har**der to** toot, or
To tutor two tutors **to** toot?

EXERCISE: 4

This one gets a laugh every time I do it and is always a hit with high school students as they wait in delicious anticipation for me to mess up. (For the record, I'm very careful when in front of students and haven't embarrassed myself yet!)

I've been doing it for more than 20 years so it rolls off my tongue at lightning speed . . . and it never gets old.

I'm a mother pheasant **pl**ucker
I **pl**uck mother pheasants
I'm the most pleasan**t** mother pheasan**t pl**ucker
Tha**t** ever **pl**ucke**d** a mother pheasant.

You may think little problems in articulation are just that: little things. But little things, over time, become part of your natural speaking pattern, your natural speaking voice. That means that your natural delivery depends on whether you practice good speech habits or allow your bad speech habits to rule.

To paraphrase the Dalai Lama: "If you think little things don't matter, try sleeping with a mosquito."

In order to communicate more clearly and effectively, you want to refine your speech patterns by practicing better speech habits.

Now that you have worked on a few exercises I hope you understand a little more about enunciation. Before we move on, it is important to point out that different rooms and different venues require different enunciation and articulation.

Enunciation and Acoustics

Rooms with a lot of steel, stone or glass are an acoustic heaven for singers and musicians. For speakers, however, they present the ultimate challenge, especially when using a microphone. In a space like that, you will need to slow down, enunciate clearly, and listen to how your voice carries.

These types of spaces have nothing to absorb sound, only reverberate it back, which means the spoken voice will get lost. If you were to speak at your typical pace, by the time those in the back heard your words, you would already be onto the next phrase and it would be jumbled and hard to listen to.

Perhaps you were in a gymnasium or a large conference room where the speaker was using the microphone but you still had a hard time comprehending her words. It's almost always because the speaker is not used to the acoustics of that particular space and doesn't know how to modify and adapt.

The complete opposite of that would be recording in a studio. Recording studios are heavily padded with acoustic panels designed to absorb sound. This is perfect for speaking, but it does present different challenges. When working on-camera or doing voice-over work be aware that over-articulating will sound ridiculous. In that case, you need to tone down and really use vocal control.

The use of pauses when recording is also entirely different from speaking in a big cavernous space. When recording in a studio, pauses have to be shorter because there is no reverberation. Too long of a pause will seem like you forgot what you were going to say and creates dead air. The same goes for speeches in small meeting rooms.

Bottom line: You will use different vocal techniques in small, more intimate presentations than you will use speaking in front of hundreds, or thousands of people.

8

YOUR BETTER VOICE

Each of us is born with a certain vocal quality which is unique. Did you know, according to the National Center for Voice and Speech[5] that no two voices are alike?

Our vocal quality includes tone, intonation, pitch, volume, breathiness, and a number of other elements. This vocal quality is our unique vocal "footprint" which assures us that, when we call up the friend we haven't talked to in 10 years, we'll only need to say their name and they will instantly recognize us.

Your tone of voice is *how* you say what you say. This is the overall quality of your voice and it determines how pleasant you are to listen to and how engaging you are as a speaker. Tone includes things like emotion or sarcasm which add meaning to your words.

Intonation, then, is how you *use your voice,* how it rises and falls while speaking. Perhaps you've heard words like inflection, timbre, cadence or lilt – those are all synonyms for intonation.

Our own vocal quality is determined by anatomical and biological factors (i.e. genetics, the length of the pharynx) as well as sociological factors (i.e. our upbringing or location.) But, aside from those of you who have taken singing or acting lessons, most people never consciously work on their vocal quality so it's just whatever they've picked up over the last few decades.

In order to really work on your vocal quality, I'm going to outline a few things here. If you need extra help, though, this is where one-on-one coaching is essential because you need to have someone with a trained ear to help you identify your areas of strength and weakness.

Some vocal issues can be easily remedied while others may take weeks, or even months, in order to create a new habit of speech. Regardless of the challenge, if you're coachable at all, you can improve.

Our individual vocal qualities are on a spectrum and so even though you may not feel you have a very rich voice, it may still be very pleasant to listen to. You would need someone – a coach – who can listen carefully to you, identify any problematic speech patterns, and determine if this should be an area you need to improve.

As you might expect from someone who has gone through vocal training and coached others on speaking, I pay attention to vocal quality. My husband and I met through Match.com so I actually heard his voice before I met him in person. His voice was part of the attraction for me and yet, he admitted to me that he had never liked his voice at all! I told him he was crazy and he had an excellent speaking voice. He didn't believe me at first. After some time of doing videos for our business and watching himself on camera, he started to hear what I did.

You see, he had developed a skewed filter through which he heard himself. After encouragement from someone he trusted, that old way of listening gave way to new ears, so to speak.

I, on the other hand, used to love my voice. My speech days were kind to me in terms of praise from judges and fellow contestants. When I got to college I was cast in a mainstage production my freshman year and continued to win roles so I was pretty confident in my vocal quality.

I was in rehearsal for a show one day and the director (who had *also* cast me in a voiceover role) walked towards me with a huge grimace on his face. He said "Leah, you sometimes get this awful Hoosier twang . . ." and he trailed off letting that hang in the air.

He had never mentioned it before, and after the initial sting of the criticism had passed, I started listening more closely to myself – and he was right!

Who would tell me that other than a theatre professor? My family? No, because they all sound like I do. Friends? Nope, they have their own accents and issues and certainly aren't trained to pick apart my voice.

It took this professor to really call me out on something so that I could be aware of it and do something about it. Do I still have a Hoosier twang after 20 years in Illinois? Yeah, I think I actually do. It only bothers me when I'm paying close attention to my voice, which usually happens when I'm recording a video.

Just because you do (or don't) like your voice doesn't mean that is how the rest of the world hears you. You need objective feedback. If you have bad vocal habits, you do need someone who can draw your attention to them so you can correct them. But sometimes, you just need encouragement.

Now that I've divulged my biggest vocal quality weakness, let's move on and help you!

The reason you want to work on your vocal quality is that the richer your voice, typically the more pleasant you will be to listen to. The more variation you add to your voice, the more dynamic you'll sound. This is one of the keys to becoming an engaging speaker.

Think of those actors or actresses who narrate animated films. They create the character simply by using interesting vocal patterns.

I suggest you watch several cartoons or animated movies but don't *watch* them. Rather, I want you to listen and notice how the voice of each character rises and falls, laughs, squeals, stutters, and gasps. It is the actor's mastery over their vocals which brings a two-dimensional cartoon to life.

After you've listened to at least one animated movie, grab a handful of your children's books or check out several of your old favorites at the library and get ready for some seriously fun practice.

EXERCISE: The Great Kids' Entertainer

When my nephew was about three, he was pretty squirmy and being the over-achieving aunt, I wanted to keep him entertained, which for me, meant being the best story-teller he'd ever heard. I put my whole body into reading Dr. Seuss' *The Foot Book*. "Left foot, Left foot, Right foot, Right foot." Along with ridiculously exaggerated movements with my feet, my voice swept up and down ("lilted") according to what I felt was necessary to keep him captivated.

No monotone here, oh no! I wouldn't read any word the same. If inflection went up on one word, it went down on the next. No two words were alike and with my animated features, Nathan would giggle, and my heart would swell just a little.

I realize you're not reading this book to entertain your kids more effectively, although that would be a nice side benefit.

What I need to be sure I'm articulating here is that you have to practice these things in a setting where you are free to experiment, where you are free to be ridiculous so you can find your better voice.

Get started – read the books as enthusiastically as you can! (You can do it alone, or – preferably – read to your kids if you have them.)

Here's the secret: once you learn how to exaggerate inflection just as you would while reading to little children, then you will begin to feel the difference. After some time, hopefully, you will begin to *hear* the difference. That's when you'll be able to take the next step of toning things down for a regular audience, retaining just enough energy to keep them not just interested, but engaged!

Regardless of whether we're reading to children or speaking in front of an audience, don't we all want them to be hanging on to our every word? As speakers, we want our audiences listening closely and we want to leave them wanting more!

9

EASY AS CONVERSATION

Speakers who focus more on themselves than on the audience will just make themselves self-conscious and nervous. How do you avoid this? The simple answer is to create a conversation.

The obvious no-no: don't talk down to your audience. It doesn't matter how little they know about the topic or how much you know. Avoid being patronizing, accusatory or a know-it-all.

The most effective speeches I've heard are those where the speaker has *created a conversation*. Certainly, not all circumstances call for engaging the audience in banter, but you *can* draft your speech in such a way that it emerges as – or simply feels – more *conversational*, rather than *presentational*.

One of your primary objectives when public speaking is to create a rapport with your audience, to connect with them. Your tone and your content work together in this regard. A conversational tone helps draw people into your world. It puts you on more of a level playing field and makes you more accessible and therefore more likable.

If you become too intent on simply getting the information in your head into an audible form to be "delivered" you will lose this crucial conversational tone. You become "directive." This often happens when you're trying too hard or trying to "sell" an idea.

At best you will come across as a novice in speaking, and quite possibly, in your field. At worst, you will come across as pompous and even adversarial. Drop whatever perceived power you think you have by virtue of having been asked to speak, and simply figure out what will resonate with your audience.

Whether you run the company and think you know better, or you think you have the Great Idea which will save the world, it doesn't matter! Your message will never be heard and your brilliance will never be realized unless you figure out how to create a conversation in which your audience wants to participate.

Once the listener feels he is being sold, or being told to do something, the dialogue, and therefore the conversation is over.

10

CREATING THE TEXT

But is it as simple as "speaking well?" No!

Ever done this for a laugh? You say to your pet, "Oh, you are the worst dog in the world, you are the absolute worst" in the sweetest possible voice and your pup wags his tail enthusiastically and looks at you with unbridled love in his eyes.

Now, of course, your audience isn't a dog – but we all know it's possible to "sweet talk" people. The text of your message must be as fully palatable as your vocal method of delivery.

As you write your speech or presentation, be sure you're keeping your audience in mind. Here are a few questions you need to ask when writing your address:

- Is my audience expecting a lecture or a conversation?
- How well-educated is my audience on this subject?
- Do I have any content that will alienate part of the group and if so, how do I address this head on?

The last piece to this is understanding how to use language to your advantage. Writing something to be read is different than writing something which is to be presented orally. Some things read well on paper but sound awkward when spoken. Pull out your thesaurus and find alternatives.

If you have to write what you'll be presenting, be sure you practice it out loud so you don't stumble or sound stilted.

While recording the audio version of my first book, *Marketing Chomp*, there were several chapters where I needed to improvise because what I had written just didn't sound right when reading out loud. I had to modify the text for the listening audience. You may need to do this too, which is why I harp on practicing out loud. You can't rely on reviewing things in your head. It just isn't the same.

Formatting Notes

If you use notes don't just print out your 12pt font, single-spaced, Word document because you're going to have a heck of a time finding where you are when you're half-way through your presentation and forget your next point.

Make it easier on yourself. Try the following:

- Double-space
- Use 16 pt. or larger font
- Use Bullet Points
- Highlight key information or critical points

I like to have my notes in outline form and then I highlight in yellow those main things I do not want to forget under any circumstance. This makes it very easy to pause and glance down at my notes to see if I've covered everything I wanted to tell my audience.

If the font is small or typed as though for an essay, it will take me too long to find my place and figure out what I had missed.

If you tend to have more of a photographic memory those bright yellow highlighted points ensure that you won't forget them because you'll see them in your mind's eye and will probably never need your notes. However, you want to be prepared. A question from the audience or an outside distraction can derail the train of thought of even a seasoned speaker. Notes are a backup at the very least.

When putting together your material be sure to prepare an outline that will help lead you to a thoughtful, relevant, interesting and organized speech.

Avoid an excessively long introduction. You want to get to the meat of your presentation sooner rather than later. After you've stated your main points, be sure to create a summary or conclusion.

Language

Let's talk about language. You know. "Language."

First, using coarse language illuminates a limited vocabulary. Second, profanity offends people during a speech even if they aren't bothered by it one-on-one. There's just something very jarring when a speaker spews it from a stage or the front of a room.

In any type of formal presentation or formal event, I recommend avoiding even the softer versions like "bull", "crap", "frickin" and "freakin." Even if you don't see anything wrong with them, there are people who still consider this crass language. The other thing that can happen is that it can sound like you're holding back on purpose, which then feels disingenuous.

Swearing isn't necessary. You don't need it at all to be an effective speaker. In fact, because the use of obscenities is so common, not hearing them can be quite refreshing.

It's a good idea to start training yourself in your everyday speech so it doesn't come out inadvertently. Instead of saying, "That was a crappy thing to do," try saying, "That was an inconsiderate thing to do."

Opting to use words that more precisely define our thoughts also improves our ability to communicate. In the previous example, you could use any of the following words in place of "crappy": shoddy, nasty, unpleasant, shabby, lousy, or rude. Sure, it's easy to use the ubiquitous "crappy," but there are so many other fabulous words in the English language why not use them?

Certainly, there are exceptions to every rule. Tony Robbins uses profanity as part of Neuro-Linguistic Programming (NLP). He can make it work, but he also creates his own speaking events. If you're relying on others to bring you in or to hire you as a guest speaker, you need to meet their standards.

And yes, I know you've read the articles saying there was a study which said people who use bad language are more "real" or are considered "more authentic." But remember what we learned about studies and surveys in Chapter 1? The results aren't always reported accurately.

Based on my experience, I will tell you that for every person who agrees that vulgar language makes you more real, there is a person who believes it makes you sound less intelligent. Remember, this book is about avoiding the pain of public speaking. Your job as a speaker is to relate to your audience and deliver your message so that it is heard and accepted. Turning off half of your audience won't accomplish that.

Ultimately, I'm going to leave you with this: if you must use coarse language, let it be with purpose, not because it slipped out.

Using Acronyms

This very last piece of content advice is something I cannot stress enough: do not use acronyms without explanations.

When you need to use acronyms, always say what they stand for first, followed by the acronym. (This is where a whiteboard or note handouts may be helpful.)

The level of sophistication of your audience doesn't matter; there is always someone who is going to be new to your group lingo or industry jargon.

I was in one high-level meeting years ago and the topic of "kegger" kept coming up. I wasn't exactly a newbie in the industry, but I was new to this particular division of the company. I couldn't figure out what the heck these people were talking about. Everything in front of me looked like financials; but what in the world was the issue with this "kegger?"

For those of you just as in the dark as I was, they weren't saying "kegger" as in fraternity parties but they were referring to Compound Annual Growth Rate or "CAGR". Urgh.

My brain never made that leap.

If you were to present financials in front of a group, you would simply say something like, "Let's look at the Compound Annual Growth Rate, or 'kegger,' as seen on page three of your handout."

Best practices would call for you to intermittently use both the full term and the acronym throughout your presentation. If you'll be speaking at length, you can eventually just use the acronym, but you need to have told your audience the meaning of the full term at least three times.

Sometimes acronyms don't just alienate an audience member, but can also cause confusion and really change the context of what you're saying.

Let's say you were telling your audience that you brought back a magazine clip from the NRA show. If your audience assumed you were at the National Restaurant Association show, they would expect you to talk about an article you clipped from a foodie magazine. However, if they thought you meant the National Rifle Association show, they would expect you to talk about the magazine clip for your firearm.

Always, always give the full meaning of all acronyms to your audience.

11

CONTENT WITH INTEGRITY

When using quotes or anecdotes, you have two options and only two options.

The first, and the one I personally follow, is to give credit. "One of my favorite Zig Ziglar quotes is . . .", or "Aristotle's thought on . . . ." You get the idea.

The second option is to assume that there are some universal thoughts, ideas, and themes that are so well-known and which have been passed on from thought-leaders for generations that they're part of the cultural fabric. Do your research and you will learn who should get the attribution. If you cannot find the original source but find that everyone seems to refer to the concept, then you're probably free to use it without citing the source, but don't try to pass it off as your original thought. There are people who are very well-read and once you try to claim another person's work as your own, you will never have any credibility with them – ever. The safest approach is to use the universal "they," as in: "They say . . . ." This lets your audience know you're not taking credit for something that isn't yours.

Let me repeat, in case you glossed over it: *don't pass someone else's idea off as your own*. Passing off someone else's content as your own is plagiarism – plain and simple. You will be caught, you will be called out and – in many cases – you will be sued for violating copyrights (so for those of you who think the internet means free reign of ideas, consider yourself warned.)

But the legal ramifications aren't even the worst, or furthest reaching, professional aspect of the problem. Nothing will undermine your credibility and your intelligence more than taking credit for something that your audience knows is not yours – and it will come back to haunt you again and again. It's naive to think no one will notice. Someone in your audience will know.

And even that isn't the worst of it.

Claiming ownership of something you didn't create is wrong. At that moment, as a person, you have something to hide. You will always be wondering who knows and who the one will be to find you out.

That deception and that paranoia will be palpable. People may not know why they don't like you, but they'll know something is "off." This sort of behavior kills your credibility as an authority on anything.

A few years ago a young speaker had what I surmise was his "big chance" to speak and probably his time to shine in front of his boss. My husband and I were there to support him, and as he started out I could tell he was nervous. But I was there just to listen.

As he continued, however, something started sounding oddly familiar. Then, I realized that I had heard this – word for word from another speaker.

At no time did he give credit to or acknowledge his source, or explain that he'd used it as inspiration. No, he had the audacity to memorize it word for word and even passed off the examples as his own revelations, saying things like, "just last week I realized" and "while I was sitting there I . . . ."

Did he think we were all stupid? Did he assume everyone was living under one big rock? Or maybe it was a moment of desperation and self-doubt that led him to believe he could get away with it and no one would care? Maybe he believed it was OK because he wasn't being paid? I'll never know.

But what I do know is that, by the end, he had zero credibility with me. Integrity is everything, and he made one of the most egregious speaker's errors, in my mind, that you can commit: blatantly stealing and passing off someone else's work as his own. The utter definition of plagiarism.

There are ways to present information with your own spin, with your own life experience. It doesn't matter how young you are. All he had to do was quote the creator of the work, or tell us he had memorized it as a learning tool. He could have referenced it as the overarching theme and used his own examples. There were a dozen different ways he could have used that material and still made it his own. But he took the lazy way out.

Don't be lazy. Sit down in a quiet space and use all eight wonderful pounds of that brain of yours.

You can augment and illustrate your points with your own life experience. You can draw from the world around you – fully cited, of course! How you make these choices is the unique perspective you can provide your audience.

Once you cross over into the territory of being paid to speak, you must take the highest road. You must use your own content or pay royalties and/or licensing fees.

The only exemption is "fair use" which is the only defense against copyright infringement. Fair Use[6] means copying material for a limited purpose, such as to comment on, criticize, or parody the original copyrighted work.

I know everybody feels they have to be the expert now. We can no longer just know what we know. People are straining to become famous, or become "somebody" and they're taking this expert thing way too far by always trying to one-up the next guy. They make stuff up because they think we, the target audience, will fall for it.

I understand these people are just trying to carve out their niche. I really don't think they mean to cause harm, but that doesn't justify the behavior.

So, if you want to be a better-than-average speaker, then accept that you're saying, in effect, "Listen to me and let me show you the way" on this or that subject. That, in turn, means you need to be a better-than-average person. Keep your integrity intact.

12

AVOID THE CRUTCH

I hate PowerPoint. I really do. It isn't that I have anything against the actual software, I just hate that it has become a crutch for speakers.

Every time I see the back of a speaker's head as they talk to the screen, I inwardly groan.

Every time a speaker reads every bullet point word for blasted word, I want to scream.

PowerPoint is not, and should not be, the focus of any presentation, ever. Unless of course, you're a teacher or professor; I'll maybe concede in those two instances only.

For the rest of you, PowerPoint is not your crutch for when you forget what you're going to say next – that's what notes are for.

The primary purpose of PowerPoint is to serve as a visual aid. It can help keep your audience engaged by giving people something else to look at other than you. It is there to show charts and graphs not easily explained verbally. It provides visual structure to a presentation but, it should not contain verbatim everything you're going to tell your audience. It should not *be* the presentation. Otherwise, *you* wouldn't be needed.

Don't turn your back to your audience to find your place in your presentation. In smaller rooms where the screen is immediately behind you and you will be standing near the projector, set up your laptop so that it is facing you. This way you can see what the audience sees without craning your neck or turning around. In larger venues, they can set this up for you even if the projector is mounted on the ceiling or further away from you, but you may need to request this configuration ahead of time.

I'll go as far as to say you can glance at the screen behind you to make sure everything is rendering properly but do it sparingly. Please don't ever read off of the screen, leaving your back or even the back of your head, facing your audience.

One exception to this would be if you have a video embedded in your presentation. In this case, you may want to turn and face the video while it is playing as a cue to the audience where they should direct their focus.

As I write this I anticipate some of the "Yeah, but's" coming my way. The reality is that some of you are going to be in situations where you have to play by someone else's rules, as problematic as they may be.

When I worked for a corporation, my peers and I had to provide sales numbers and marketing data to management, and we were required to submit slides prior to the meeting. In that case, yes, we did have to cram too much information onto slides. There are times you may also need to break the rules of common sense, or best-practices, in order to keep the peace or your job.

When you are in complete control:

- Use large font for those in the back row
- Use phrases instead of whole sentences
- Use two, or even three slides, instead of jamming too much content onto one slide

One reason you don't want all of the detail of what you're going to say on your slides is simply that you will have fast readers in your audience. They will have read through your entire slide by the time you've finished your first bullet point. What happens then? They will get bored because you aren't giving them any content they can't read for themselves.

Use your slides as an outline and as an overview of your main points. You, as the speaker, should be providing all the juicy details.

The Basics of PowerPoint Are:

- Keep the slides simple and clean
- Don't use overly complicated design templates
- Use big enough font to be seen from several feet away
- Avoid yellows and pastels which are washed out on screen

The only way to determine the viability of your visuals is to view them in full presentation mode, from the distance that your farthest audience member might be sitting.

Practically speaking you're not always going to fully know about the slides' effectiveness, and I realize there are sometimes charts and graphs wherein the detail is just not going to show up. That's the kind of circumstance where you use a pointer and clear, concise explanations.

Good practice for presenters is to have your PowerPoint available as a PDF document for your audience. You can email it to the event organizer to disseminate to the audience after the event or at least have it available for anyone who asks for it.

In certain situations, you may want your audience to have a paper copy of your presentation as you're talking. Anytime you give people material ahead of time, you must weigh the pros and cons of doing so. The upside is that they can take notes on the pages relevant to the content. The downside is that you will hear rustling paper and will have people who will work ahead. The sound of all those flipping pages can be a distraction.

You have to determine the structure and overall tone you want. If you're teaching and you're in a workshop setting, you will probably want your audience to have something in order to follow the content.

If your audience really doesn't need the slides, try creating a worksheet or two, where they can fill in answers as they follow along. Worksheets are especially valuable when you create them in such a way that the audience can fill in key take-aways.

Another option would be to hand out notes periodically throughout the presentation, which also has its pros and cons. An audience can't get ahead of you, but this can cause a disruption and down-time. On the flip side, it can be a chance to break up boredom and give a little respite – depending on how long your talk is. Perhaps a single page outline/highlights would be more appropriate. It all depends on the venue, the audience, the length of presentation, and the purpose.

In settings like classes, seminars, and workshops, audiences love to receive printed examples, exercises, or other supporting documentation. It helps them remember what they've learned and gives them something they can take with them.

PowerPoint is no longer your only option. You might want to try Prezi or Slidebean instead. But, don't misunderstand my basic point. It isn't the software that is the problem. It is how speakers use the software.

Use slide software the way it was meant to be used and it will do what it's meant to do: enhance your public speaking event.

13

PERFECT PRACTICE

Not practicing is a surefire way to remain nervous and make your audience uneasy. Why? Because it's painful to watch nervous speakers. No one likes watching someone in an uncomfortable situation because it makes us, the audience, uncomfortable.

The more you practice, the more you'll be able to control any nerves and come across more polished, even if you do have clammy hands and butterflies.

We've heard it since we were kids, "practice makes perfect." But not if we practice wrong! Believe it or not, there are *right* ways and there are *wrong* ways to practice.

My mom had a technique for the moment a practicing student would mess up: she would stop them and make them start over. Her theory was that you shouldn't practice your mistakes. Made sense to me even then. Years later I read *The Talent Code* by Daniel Coyle and discovered that science has now backed up what my mom knew all along – there is such a thing as *perfect* practice! Coyle calls it "deep practice."

I have found there are three basic types of practice:

Practice for Memory

Memorizing word for word comes into play when we're rehearsing the lines of a script for a commercial, theatre or television production, or a short speech where having notes would be distracting. If we're practicing a script we have to keep the integrity of the author's writing; if it's an introduction we need to make sure we get names, dates, and information correct.

When you need to practice in order to memorize, you must rely on *repetition*. In order to efficiently memorize your material, begin by reading through the material out loud several times. Shortly, you'll be breaking the text into small chunks, so these first few readings are important to get a sense of the whole text.

After you've completed reading the entire material out loud, set your pages aside – but within reach – and start practicing line by line. Start with the first sentence, say the first sentence out loud, from memory.

Then check your pages. How did you do? Did you miss a word or insert a different word? Read the entire sentence out loud again. Then, looking away, repeat it from memory.

Check your progress again. Did you nail it this time? Great! Now, include the second sentence, try saying it word for word without reading.

You'll repeat this process stringing the sentences together in groups until you can rehearse them all, in order, from memory.

This is tedious and time-consuming and there's no short-cut. This is how it's done.

If you flub up, you start from the beginning and you keep doing this until you have practiced all the way through flawlessly. This trains your brain and your tongue to get used to delivering your speech word-for-word correctly.

Let me suggest that even if you aren't memorizing an entire speech, you should at least memorize your outline and key points in case something happens where you can't rely on your notes.

One of my clients relayed an experience where she was speaking in front of a large crowd in an auditorium. Not only was the prompter not queued properly, the spotlight went out so she couldn't see her written notes. However, she managed to continue talking. In fact, her boss came in late and didn't see the light go out and had no idea she didn't have a prompter. He only heard her speech and told her she did a great job! He didn't notice the little hiccup because she had memorized her main points and was prepared.

Memory is very much like a muscle. The more you "exercise," the more you memorize material, the easier it will be. If you regularly memorize short paragraphs, soon you'll be able to memorize a page of material, and then several pages of a speech.

If you haven't done this before or have told yourself you aren't good at this, then expect to work a little harder initially. You have to practice *at practicing*. It will get easier!

Practice for Delivery

Practicing for delivery assumes that your material is already committed to memory; or, there is no requirement for you to memorize word for word. Practicing for delivery is simply working on the mechanics.

Perhaps you've been asked to be part of a panel discussion where your professional experience will be drawn upon. Since this is knowledge you can readily speak about, it's more about being able to articulate clearly rather than memorizing specific answers.

When you practice for delivery, you are primarily working on your tone of voice and articulation.

Practicing your delivery is usually more about being able to be clearly understood, and maintaining a tone and mood.

An excellent way to practice your delivery is to record yourself speaking. Listen to how you sound. Do you hear anything you haven't noticed before?

If you've never heard yourself recorded this can be a humbling experience because you will sound different than you expected. When we hear ourselves speak our inner ear is picking up on the vibrations happening in our body that an outside listener doesn't hear.

In order to be objective, we need to listen to our recorded voice so we hear ourselves without those internal vibrations. This allows us to hear our voice in the same way others hear us. Once you have recorded yourself, play it back and focus on listening to whether or not you sound natural and effortless. It can be hard to be objective at first but, the more you do this, the better you will become at evaluating and correcting yourself.

Practice for Confidence

Practicing for confidence means ensuring that you know your material and can deliver it effectively.

Practicing for confidence is paramount when you're not only delivering a spoken text but integrating visual aids (such as a PowerPoint presentation) and preparing answers to anticipated questions.

An actual script may not be necessary. In this case, you would practice reciting your key phrases and "data points" (or other information) in "chunks" so when called upon, they roll flawlessly off of your tongue.

If you practice articulating all those facts, statistics, sales numbers etc. out loud, you'll achieve confidence in that content, and it will more easily come to you when you're in front of the group.

Don't rely on just reading through your presentation. You need to actually stand up and pretend your boss is staring you down and the squirrelly sales folks are getting restless. Practice with your environment in mind – it will help you when it's actually happening.

Think of it this way: If you were to write out a product report or customer analysis which you knew your boss was going to read, wouldn't you take considerable time reviewing it? You'd read it several times, proof it, and perhaps even have a peer review it for you. In the same way you take the time to work on written documents, take the time to rehearse what you're going to say.

Too often we think we can just *wing it*. I hate to break this to you, but those witty ad-libs from professional speakers? Well, those are rehearsed. I might be breaking some cardinal rule against sharing great public speaker secrets, but it's a fact. They practice timing, inflection, and intonation. The reason it looks easy is that those who do it well, *practice*!

Tiger Woods made golf look so easy that he inspired a generation of new golfers. It's what happens when someone masters a craft. They're magicians, creating an illusion: they make it look so easy, others are provoked to action trying that thing for themselves! The reality is that it doesn't come naturally; it requires tedious hours of practice. That's how you get to be great. Yes, "off the cuff" remarks appear to be spur of the moment thoughts, *when practiced to perfection!*

Practice in front of anyone who will listen. It could be your mom, your best friend who owes you a favor, or a co-worker. Buy coffee, buy dinner – whatever it takes. If you're going to speak in front of people, you need to practice *in front of people*. You need human feedback. People cough; they get bored; they laugh. They'll give you visual clues as to where you're losing them, and they'll tell you what needs clarity. Join groups that will give you a chance to speak and that will provide feedback, like Toastmasters.

The amount of practice you need should be proportionate to the length and complexity of your presentation.

One thing to keep in mind is that whether you've been practicing 20 minutes or two weeks, at some point you will likely become tired. Once you start stumbling, fumbling and generally becoming sloppy – stop! It will do you no good to practice when you're in the wrong state of mind. You'll end up with the wrong words and the wrong pacing. You'll be *practicing wrong*.

Anything new can be tiring because you're engaging your entire system in learning; and it's no different in public speaking. Your throat may get dry, you may start to feel emotionally drained or burned out.

Walk away, go to bed. Take some type of break. You may only need a few minutes or you may need to wait a day. Just understand that you will reach your limit at times and that's normal.

The last point about practice pertains to the moments leading up to your presentation. You must warm up. You don't make a professional phone call as soon as you crawl out of bed in the morning (unless, on that rare occasion, you *want* your boss to hear just how awful you sound when calling in sick.) So, don't go into a speaking engagement cold.

If you start lifting weights without warming up, you will get injured eventually. If your voice isn't warmed up, you won't have control over your nerves or your breath. Your voice will sound thin and strained, not to mention that your audience will pick up on your lack of focus. They won't really "like" you, even if they don't know why.

If all of this is new to you, your warm-up will help you start recalling the points you've been practicing. You will be exercising that muscle memory.

Warming up is your last chance to prepare, your last practice. But more on that in Chapter 21.

14

CHECK YOUR PROPS

I'm using a theatre reference. A "prop" in theatre is an object whose use is specific to an individual and action, and if the production is any good, that prop is anything but superfluous. It is crucial. If it wasn't there, you'd know something was wrong.

The broader noun form of "prop" [7] literally means "a person or thing serving as *a support or stay*." Again, there is this notion of indispensability.

For our purposes, this can mean the person scheduled to introduce you, your slides, your notes, the projector remote, or anything else that will either facilitate or hinder your presentation.

Because they are so important, actors are firmly reminded to check their own props before each performance. You should also rigorously check your props before "taking the stage."

Presenters often fumble over silly things. It's happened to all of us so don't dismiss this as a no-brainer. There are no short-cuts when it comes to preparation.

Take full responsibility for anyone and everything which will be part of your presentation. Don't assume it's going to be OK. Those at the top of their game in any profession leave nothing to chance, and neither should you when it comes to speaking.

Attention to detail is what separates the beginner from the expert, and all too often even experienced speakers will take for granted that they can figure things out on the fly.

It can be irritating to watch someone futz with the remote and blame the projector. Worse still is for a speaker to blame another person for something not working as expected. Worst of all, however, is knowing that a simple check would have prevented those issues.

People hate having their time wasted. Not only is it disrespectful to the audience, but they instantly disengage when one of these mishaps flare up.

Not every projector's remote is programmed the same. If you've emailed your slides to someone ahead of time they may have inadvertently switched your slides. These things can happen any number of ways. If you're speaking, then make it your business to *check your props*.

Always Be Prepared

Be prepared. This seems so obvious, but once you start paying attention, you'll be amazed how many speakers act as if they never thought they'd be in front of an audience.

Have water accessible, have your notes, your pointer, and know how to operate your remote if you're using a projector. You may even ask someone else to "drive" for you (i.e. they advance the slides for you if you're using PowerPoint) if they're well-acquainted with your presentation.

Get as familiar as possible with the room in which you'll be speaking. Is there an air-conditioner or fan causing background noise? If so, you're going to have to speak louder than usual so the folks in the back of the room can hear you. Pay attention to this ahead of time so you can adjust your volume.

There are certain environments where you are likely to be asked questions that you won't be able to answer on the spot but will be expected to follow up with an answer within a few days. I'm thinking of corporate or technical presentations. It is always OK to say, "I don't know the answer to that, but I'll get back to you." But then, be sure you follow up!

Assign someone else to take notes or jot down questions. Don't drop your focus to scribble down a note to follow up on something because here's what will happen:

1) You will lose your audience. Once you've dropped your focus from them, they drop their focus on you. Audiences typically perceive your divided attention as permission to strike up the conversation with their neighbor.

2) You'll likely scribble some type of shorthand that even you won't recognize later.

By asking someone else to write down the questions, you demonstrate that you are prepared and in control. Whoever is your scribe should be able to neatly write out questions in their entirety, ensuring you'll know how to respond.

15

LET'S GET PHYSICAL

When it comes to public speaking . . . looks matter. Your clothes matter, personal hygiene matters, your hair matters, your shoes matter, your tone of voice matters, your attitude matters, your character matters, it all matters!

You always want to be a little better put-together than your audience. Things like wrinkled clothes, falling hems, scruffy shoes, rumpled papers – all will detract from your presentation and erode your professionalism.

But wait, you ask, doesn't all this conflict with being "me" in front of the room? Remember earlier when I wrote that you should be you – only better? Being authentic does not mean wearing the same clothes in which you run around doing errands. Being a public speaker means you do have to dress the part.

Notice I didn't say *play* the part. This isn't acting, this is you – at your absolute best.

Suits are almost always appropriate. They make you look professional and pulled together. There's no reason to go overboard; buy what you can afford. The most important thing is to find one that makes you look and feel fantastic!

There are times when it is appropriate to be more informal, but you need to know your audience and the venue. When in doubt, opt for the suit. It's always better to be a bit over-dressed rather than under-dressed.

You will want to look polished from head to toe. For men, this means things like shaving the hair on the back of your neck, taking care of facial grooming and polishing your shoes. For women, this means keeping your hair neat and wearing heels that haven't been chewed up by the pavement.

Eye Contact

Make eye contact and allow yourself (or force yourself!) to really connect with your audience. I know this can be intimidating or scary for some of you, but it really separates the novice from the expert speaker. If you're not used to doing this, it will be difficult at first. But, it is absolutely essential to master this important skill. The more you do it, the easier it will become.

I actually saw a speaker giving instructions to an audience on public speaking and she didn't make eye contact while talking about "eye contact!" How credible do you think she was to her audience?

Remember, your audience is there to listen to you and they expect you to connect with them. The easiest way to connect with them is to make eye contact.

Sincerity

Everything in personal relationships and business really comes down to this: you have to be sincere. You can be in front of a room of a hundred people and shaking with nerves, but if you are sincere, your audience will extend grace. You can also be a very dry presenter, but if you're genuine and your audience can relate to you and feels a rapport with you, they'll forgive your less-than-entertaining presentation skills.

I wish this were a given, but it isn't. There are far too many people out there who are determined to keep the world from seeing the "real" them. They still believe that people like them better as robotic versions of themselves. They're wrong, but that just leaves more room for those authentic souls to rise up to be the best in their respective fields.

Be Relatable

Several years ago my husband and I attended a nutrition workshop held by a doctor who had a pretty amazing health story. Unfortunately, his presentation was tainted for me because he had made an error in judgment in his choice for the person opening up that day.

The majority of attendees were overweight with visible aches and pains. Several attendees had problems simply walking from the door to the chairs.

The young woman who kicked off the workshop was incredibly skinny. Not just slender or thin, but the 90-pounds-soaking-wet kind of skinny.

She gave the welcoming speech and lectured us to make better choices. That part was fine, who can't benefit from that kind of challenge once in a while? Here's where it spiraled downhill for me: she proceeded to tell us that if *she* could lose 5 pounds then so could everyone in the audience.

I'll let that sink in for a moment.

Someone who had zero weight struggles lecturing a group of people, many of whom were obese, on weight loss. I wasn't even there for weight loss but I felt judged and actually discouraged rather than encouraged.

This is more than just knowing your audience, this is about understanding your relationship with them and how you will be perceived. You must not only know your audience but relate to them. You also need to be sensitive to situations which can be emotionally charged.

When you are in front of a room you will have a certain amount of power as the speaker. Prepare ahead of time. Choose your words wisely.

Enthusiasm

Did you ever have a teacher or professor who seemed bored by their own material? How well did you listen? Did you learn anything? If you're like most of us, you tune out if the *speaker* isn't even excited.

On the flip side, have you ever heard someone talk on a rather dry topic who made it utterly fascinating simply because of how excited they were? That's exactly what I'm talking about. Be assured that, whatever you're speaking about, enthusiasm is contagious so, whatever you're sharing with your audience . . . be excited!

There is, however, a caveat.

One of my early supervisors told me, during employee evaluations, that I could make a bad idea sound good because I would present it so enthusiastically.

At first, I took it as a compliment. As I digested it over the next few days, however, I realized that it wasn't a good trait if I was to build trust and continue to climb the corporate ladder. I needed to learn to be more discerning about which ideas I supported. From then on, I began to apply more critical thinking.

In public speaking, you want to earn and build trust with your audience. Good, strong, positive energy certainly helps. But, being overly zealous can actually work against you.

You want to bring enthusiasm and excitement at an appropriate level for your particular audience.

Move Like a Pro

There are many venues and circumstances where standing still behind a lectern is your only viable option. There's nothing wrong with that. However, when you do have the opportunity to move, then, by all means, take advantage of it.

Movement (including gestures, or walking around while you're speaking) can be a tricky area to coach without seeing how you naturally move. Some people are naturally more graceful than others and will look confident in front of a room, even if they're nervous. Others will look nervous because of how they move, even if they're inwardly calm. There isn't a right or wrong way to move *per se*; rather, it's going to be based on you and what feels natural to you.

Walking around the room or stepping off of a stage can be fantastic ways to engage your audience. This is especially important in workshop or seminar settings where you're interacting with the audience. When someone asks a question, walk toward that side of the room.

If you have only stood behind a lectern or have stood motionless and haven't explored what it feels like to move around, I think you'll be pleasantly surprised at how much better it will feel as a speaker. I'm betting that, once you practice a bit, you'll feel more at ease than standing still. If you move naturally, it will also be more visually interesting for your audience.

This is where watching yourself on video is the most helpful. Record yourself and then watch for nervous habits like rocking back and forth, wringing your hands or excessively touching your face or hair. These are all "self-soothing" movements and will tend to convey to the audience that you're ill at ease.

You might find that you pace, or constantly shift your weight from side to side. There are as many nervous tics as there are individuals. Some are simply distracting, while others can actually agitate your audience.

Are you a pacer when you're nervous? Pacing creates a frenetic energy that your audience can feel. It's better to keep yourself in one spot than to pace back and forth.

Evaluate how you stand. Is your weight on one leg or evenly dispersed? When we shift our weight to one side (or, worse, from side to side) it can take away some of our authority.

One speaker I knew was struggling to develop his confidence in front of a room. When he was unsure of himself he shifted his weight to his right leg. When I got him talking about something for which he had passion, I noticed he naturally centered his weight which contributed to a more confident delivery. What's more, his voice even took on a more confident tone. Once I pointed this out, he then had a tool to use. When his weight was centered he was in more of a power pose and it affected his delivery in a very positive way.

Most of us have quirks we don't notice until someone points them out. That's why it's helpful to practice in front of people and watch yourself on video. It can be uncomfortable at first, but it works. It doesn't matter how experienced you are at public speaking, watching yourself every once in a while is important. You may be fidget-free for years only to suddenly start, without even being aware of it. You may conquer one bad habit only to trade it for another.

We typically make these unconscious movements when we're nervous or uncomfortable, but that doesn't mean it's limited to just those who are apprehensive about speaking in front of people. Any type of unconscious movement can be triggered by simply being in front of a larger crowd than normal or not being as prepared as usual.

Sometimes simply holding an object takes away that uneasiness because there's a sort of barrier between speaker and audience. Hand someone a pen and they no longer feel as vulnerable in front of a room. It might sound weird, but I've seen it work!

If you know you tend to pace, rock, wring your hands or are otherwise restless, then put a plan in place. Ask for a lectern where your hands will have a place to rest, or try holding a tablet for your notes (and yes, notes are perfectly acceptable). Find what works best for you.

16

OWN YOUR ROOM

One of the easiest ways to set yourself apart as an experienced and polished speaker is how well you handle a room.

We all know first impressions are critical and yet it's quite common for speakers to lose their audience before they even speak.

How do you avoid this?

Own the Room.

To take a bit of liberty with the phrase attributed to Martin Luther King Jr., "You are not the thermometer – you are the thermostat." In other words, you monitor and control the room.

So – what are some of the ways we do this?

Know When to be Quiet

One of my biggest pet peeves is missing a person's name because the speaker is self-conscious and feels compelled to start speaking as soon as they're in front of the room, even though people are still talking or the applause has not died down.

The amateur speaker starts talking before people are ready. The professional waits until the people are ready and *owns the room*.

You've heard it in terms of interviewing and negotiating: *know when to be quiet*. This knowledge is also important when it comes to owning a room.

It all starts from the moment you step up in front of the room. You need to command attention. Don't start speaking until everyone has settled down, stopped talking *and* all eyes are on you.

There is no need for strained yelping for people to quiet down. You, as the speaker, need to remain calm, poised, pleasant, alert – in short, happy to be there. Those paying attention will give you their undivided attention but don't let that be enough.

People who are paying attention will see that you're quietly waiting and will become annoyed with those delaying your start and they will take care of the shushing for you.

Don't believe me? If you've ever taken a negotiating class, or read anything on interviewing, then you surely also know that there are times when silence is golden and the person who speaks first is in the weaker position. So it is here.

I developed my understanding and affection for this method back in high school. At speech meets there was always that one judge who was never quite ready. He or she would be looking for a pen, or shuffling through papers and not watching the beginning of the contestant's presentations. This bothered me and I told my coach (my mom) about it. Her response was, "Well, just look at them until they feel your eyes boring into them and don't start until you have their attention!"

After her pep talk, when I would go to the front of the room and had a judge who wasn't looking at me, I waited. And waited. The judge, noticing a longer than usual silence, would look around and discover I was waiting for his or her attention. Then I would receive a sheepish nod indicating that I could start.

That judge would miss my competitors first few lines, but they never missed mine! I was sold on it when I saw how it gave me much better control and command of the room.

By the way, this isn't just for competitive speech presentations, I've also used this technique in other instances, such as when presenting at sales meetings in front of top executives. I did it to control the room. Try it sometime – it really works!

Stop being afraid of standing without speaking. The audience's attention is the very least you should expect. If you don't value yourself, your time, or your content enough to care about the first words out of your mouth, you immediately undermine your own value.

If you're the highlight of a program, or your product is deserving of the spotlight, then you should give yourself the credit which is due. You should always expect more than the average presenter. Expect *everyone's* attention!

You can also augment this kind of command right from the beginning by having someone introduce you. Instead of standing next to them, stand off to the side of the room. Far enough away that the audience's full attention is on them. Once they have completed their introduction, they look over at you, and you start walking to your position over the applause. Once you're in front, you wait until the applause is finished and then you speak.

Engaging the Audience

We've talked a lot about how you, the speaker, ward off problems – defensive driving of the event, as it were.

Now, there's another aspect to this: going out on a limb and *engaging* your audience, actively inviting them into the mix with questions or other means.

You can ask questions in the very beginning to learn more about your audience. For example, "How many business owners do we have in the audience today? How many marketing professionals are here?" Questions like this can help you determine the mix of the group.

In the training workshops we hold, these questions help us give relevant examples to that particular audience.

Asking questions throughout your program can keep your audience engaged and can make it more fun for you. I often hear from public speaking clients that just asking questions calms their nerves. Why? Because the focus is no longer on themselves!

When you shift your focus on to your audience, you won't be worried about yourself. This is an excellent way to engage your audience while also decreasing your anxiety.

17

EDIFYING

This is a term many people aren't familiar with and when I first heard it in relation to introducing a speaker, it made perfect sense.

"To instruct or benefit, especially morally or spiritually; uplift."[8]

That last definition, "uplift," that's rather beautiful, isn't it? Don't you want someone to uplift you, to elevate you, before your audience?

Setting up a speaker is incredibly important in terms of how the audience responds. If someone quickly mumbles an introduction for a speaker and the speaker walks up, it's a bit ho-hum. But, when there is an impressive introduction it floods the room with anticipation.

As a speaker, you should have a prepared introduction that highlights who you are without it being overly wordy or overly flattering. It needs to contain a brief bio, including pertinent credentials that indicate why you're qualified to be speaking, and maybe one or two fun-facts to help the audience relate to you.

I recommend having your introduction typed up in large-font and double-spaced to make it easy to read for the person introducing you. (Refer back to Chapter 10 for a refresher on how to prepare your notes.) Email them a copy ahead of time and be sure to take a copy with you to every event in case the person introducing you didn't print it out.

When you're asked to introduce a speaker, be prepared. Know who the person is and something about her. If she's given you a bio be sure you have read through it, out loud, several times. If it is not typed up in my aforementioned easy-to-read method, retype it for yourself. Oh, and be sure to clarify the pronunciation of names ahead of time! Also, if you know the speaker as "Ronnie" but she lists "Veronica" on her bio, ask for her preference.

Here are a few things to include when you are introducing and edifying someone:

- Full name
- Subject they will be talking about
- Qualifications
- A connection to an organization or the area, or another tidbit which helps the audience relate to them

When you give a proper introduction, you're giving the audience the reason why they should listen closely. In one sense, you're the opening band for the feature act. Your job is to get the audience warmed up and focused.

Even if the same courtesy was not extended to you, as a speaker yourself, always be gracious and have an edifying remark ready about any person you introduce.

Don't use inside jokes, or make your introduction overly personal.

Stick to professional comments:

> *I'm excited to introduce Jill Marketer as she'll be sharing with us the campaign for our new product line. She'll also be showing a preview of the new website her team has*

been working on so diligently these last few weeks.

It's professional, it's to the point.

If you're in a setting where you're introducing an expert, then your introduction needs to be grander:

> Mr. Sam Speaker is generously sharing his time with us today because he is passionate about helping young entrepreneurs remove barriers to success. For 13 years, Mr. Speaker has been tirelessly devoting volunteer hours to ensure that business owners have the keys to succeed. Today he is sharing with us some of the very same secrets that have helped hundreds of start-ups. Please give a warm welcome to Mr. Speaker!

If someone has traveled to speak, amp it up another level:

> We are privileged to have with us this afternoon, Ms. Sales Number of Generous Profits, Inc. She has generated unprecedented sales numbers for every division she has worked with at GPI. Ms. Number has dedicated the last four years to

serving her community by offering small businesses the kind of financial advice they wouldn't otherwise have access to. Ms. Number is someone whom I personally admire and it is my honor to introduce her. Please help give her a warm welcome, Ms. Sales Number . . . .

How would you feel going on stage, or up to the front of the room after that type of introduction? Great, right? It's all about setting the person up for success.

If you don't know the speaker personally, don't say that you do. Don't claim they are better than they are or more full of life than they are, because guess what? The audience will be disappointed and/or you will lose credibility.

I witnessed such an introduction, a speaker who we were told "lit up the room" by a man who didn't sound sincere at all. Not to mention the alleged "light" this man spoke of must've been on a dimmer switch because I didn't see it. My point is this – you have to be sincere. You have to be real. Inform, but don't overstate. Present in a positive light and you will leave a positive impression with your audience and the person you introduce.

What's the appropriate length of an introduction? I think this depends on the venue. The larger the event, the more formal the event, the longer the introduction might be. I've had to listen to lengthy bios for informal networking events which just felt contrived and left me thinking "Who cares?" Save the resume for awards dinners and similar formal presentations. Give the necessary background to set the stage for the speaker in this particular setting. Keep introductions on point and add a bit of relevant interest.

Be sure introductions are audience and room-appropriate. Being overly loud or overly enthusiastic in small rooms can come across as forced and insincere. Even in the smallest settings you can, however, build to a crescendo and ask your audience to welcome the speaker with enthusiasm. If the speaker falls flat, don't let it be because you didn't tee it up for them. Make sure you have done everything you can to set the stage for them to deliver brilliantly.

When it is you who has been introduced, be sure to give it back to the person with something like:

> *Thank you, Susie, for the warm welcome and for inviting me out here today. Susie is the*

hardest working woman I know; you are lucky to have her working on your behalf.

Keep it short, relevant, and real.

18

THE BIG DAY

First, let's talk about punctuality. Showing respect for your audience is paramount. You should arrive early, start on time and finish on time. You do not wait for others to trickle into the room. Honor those who showed up on time to hear you speak. Respect their time.

Beyond that, it's easy to avoid giving much attention to preparing ourselves for our big day, much less thinking about how we should prepare physically for public speaking. We spend time fretting about things we can't control, or worrying about whether we have the right material, enough material, and the list goes on. We should keep our focus on the things we can control and by planning ahead it puts us in the driver's seat.

Gone are the days where I look all fresh and bright-eyed on two hours of sleep. If I don't want puffy eyes, I need to be working out and getting eight hours of sleep in the days leading up to any public speaking event. Ice water and under eye concealer certainly do a lot, but they can't conceal being exhausted. Get plenty of sleep!

Hydrate. It's important for your energy and necessary to avoid dry mouth. You don't want to be in the middle of your knock-'em-dead line and start coughing uncontrollably or lose your voice. Resist the temptation, however, to slam a bunch of water the day of the speech, because that will make you feel bloated and you'll also be preoccupied with finding the closest restroom. If you're properly hydrated then your body will be on a schedule and you won't have to worry about emergencies.

Avoid eating only minutes before you speak. There are the obvious lettuce-in-the-teeth reasons and then there are the lesser known problems. Eating coats your tongue and your teeth, making your mouth feel gummy, and affecting enunciation.

Just because you're speaking at an event where you're seated at a table where a meal is being served, doesn't mean you are obligated to eat. Often meals at these functions are full of bread and low-nutrient carbs. They'll fill you up, but you will crash from all the carbs-turned-to-sugar coursing through your body. You don't want your energy to tank just when it's your time to shine.

If appropriate, you may prefer to circulate to other tables while everyone else eats so you get a sense for your audience. This allows you to focus on the reason you're there. Some speakers do this to better gauge their audience or to anticipate the type of questions they'll be asked later.

Think about where you typically speak. Watch what everyone else does who speaks – and do the opposite. That might be extreme, but my point is that very few speakers really think about what they're doing and why they're doing it. Even fewer are consciously doing things to set themselves apart. If the group is eating lunch, most speakers will gobble up the free lunch. You don't have to.

As a speaker, you should always control as much of your environment as you can and often that means going against the grain.

There are award dinners and events where you simply can't avoid eating with everyone else. In those situations, I recommend eating lightly and excuse yourself to chew gum or pop a few breath mints to clear your palate before speaking. (Peppermint is also known for its invigorating properties; just remember to spit out your gum or finish that mint before heading to the front of the room!)

If you need an even more compelling reason to avoid eating, it's because you don't know what they'll be serving. You don't want to eat something just because it's in front of you only to burp, experience rumbling digestion, or worse! – while speaking.

19

When Murphy Speaks

Things will go wrong and it's just as true in public speaking as it is in anything else. This might be the thing you fear the most about public speaking.

While it's true there are a lot of tricky situations that pop up when you are in front of a room, the more experience you gain as a speaker, the better you will become at adapting to challenges.

Distractions and Difficult People

Don't allow distractions to derail you. You don't stop for the person sticking their head in the door to drop off a message. You don't allow an audience member to speak over you. During a workshop where my husband and I were training a group of business owners, one of the men asked the same question twice in a row, even after we had addressed it the first time. After the second time, I simply said, "That's something specific to your business that we aren't covering today, let's talk afterward." I kept my tone friendly, but I was firm. I didn't pause, I quickly went to my next point shifting my focus from him to the rest of the group. Several participants later thanked me for nipping it in the bud because it wasn't relevant to the topic or anyone else in the room.

Remember, when you are speaking in front of an audience, you have an obligation to the entire group, not just one individual.

If there's a lawn mower outside, a vacuum next door, or an A/C blower that kicks on which starts to hinder your presentation, talk louder, step off of the podium, and get out from behind the lectern – whatever it takes to get closer to your audience so you will be heard.

Don't ever let something or someone hijack your presentation – your audience will appreciate your ability to overcome obstacles and maintain control over the situation.

Hecklers

One of the scariest things that can happen is to have a heckler. This isn't stand-up comedy, but it's essentially the same thing. I'm referring to an audience member who wants to draw the attention to themselves. They'll be the ones who are rude, will challenge you, or claim to know more than you do.

I was speaking to marketing peers, and at a point when I asked a question, a woman raised her hand and proceeded to speak at great length on why she didn't find anything relevant and that she was "beyond all of this." As she was talking I could see a few eye rolls coming from people in front of her, silently giving me the indication they did not agree and to not pay her any attention. There was complete silence as everyone waited for me to respond. What did I do? First of all, I agreed with her. People who aren't open-minded and who think they know everything can't be reasoned with, especially in a public setting. As a speaker, it will do you no good to become defensive or passive-aggressive.

I looked directly at her as I explained I didn't expect that anything I said would be new to her, that the point of the exercise was about the execution, the follow through and if she was already doing all of that, then great! I did this so she felt heard and received that significance she was seeking. Then I took a stronger stand and explained that the exercise is meant to get her to the next level, regardless of where she was right now. I asked if she was really satisfied with her level of success and what she was doing to get to the next level. I didn't wait for an answer, I shifted my focus to the rest of the audience, drawing them into the conversation.

I had two people immediately raise their hands to offer how they found the exercise quite useful and they explained why. It was their way of sending me some reassurance despite her criticism.

At the very end of my presentation when I was asking a few more questions of the group, I purposely directed a question to her. I did this to keep her participating and to maintain a sense of control over the entire situation.

There was quite a bit of positive that came out of it. I was an out of town guest and the rest of the group had been embarrassed by her behavior. Instant sympathy. Afterwards, people lined up to buy my book and talk to me. Several people told me how rude they thought she had been. One person told me they wouldn't be doing any future business with her because of how she had treated me. I even received praise on how well I handled the situation and how impressed they were that I actually drew her back into the conversation at the end.

The best part was the heckler herself approached me afterward in a veiled attempt to apologize, only to end up asking for me to influence one of my clients to do business with her! See, it was never about me. It was never about my content. It was about how she could try to make herself seem smarter than the featured speaker. Maybe she was jealous because she saw I had done business with a former client of hers. I don't know the depths of her dysfunction, I just know you don't ever want to take hecklers personally. Their behavior is a reflection of their character, not about you as a speaker.

Goof-Ups

Mess up? Apologize once and move on. To continually apologize undermines your confidence and your authority. The sooner you forget about it, the sooner your audience will too.

Never apologize for a lack of speaking skills, or talk about being nervous. If you're actually quite good it sounds like you're fishing for sympathy. If you aren't all that polished or are visibly nervous, you will only be stating the obvious. No need. (Remember, most of your audience is going to be far more forgiving because they're glad it's you up there and not them!)

Have you ever walked around a corner and almost bumped into someone? What is your immediate reaction? Quick, say it out loud.

If you're a woman, you very likely said, "I'm sorry." If you're a man, you most likely said, "Excuse me." Forgive any gross generalizations but I have found this to be quite true. Early in my career, a woman pointed this out to me and I started making a shift in my language.

I had to learn to stop apologizing for things that weren't my fault. This is the reason I don't like apologies from speakers. You should apologize when you have done something wrong, caused harm, or caused a person an inconvenience. Apologizing out of habit is a submissive act and there's no place for it as a speaker.

Many public speaking experts will tell you not to apologize, even if you're late. Let's be real. There is a distinct difference between acknowledging you kept your audience waiting and apologizing for a cold. If you have derailed a program because of your tardiness, a short, sincere and humble apology is in order. Everyone who has ever traveled understands airline delays and traffic. I've seen speakers turn their story into nice segues for their speeches. If you can do that, great. If not, apologize and move on.

In Sickness and Sneezing

You don't need to apologize for having a cold because your audience will hear it. Highlighting it only makes things worse. I sometimes don't even hear it in someone's voice until they apologize for being nasally. After that, my attention is divided because I'm wondering how different they would really sound if they were healthy.

If you cough, avoid saying "I'm sorry", simply say, "Excuse me" and move on. (This is another good reason to have water handy.)

If you sneeze, a simple, "excuse me" will suffice. Speaking of sneezing, you're in for a bit of trivia. Do you know what the space between your nose and upper lip is called? Not to worry, I didn't either. It's your "philtrum" and there's a very important reason to know this. If you ever feel a sneeze coming on while you're in front of people, here's an old stage trick: take your index finger and press it firmly and horizontally against your philtrum. (It looks like a finger mustache). It usually stops a sneeze dead in its tracks. Practice it and you can make it look like you're deep in thought. I have used this countless times in front of people, in meetings, in church . . . it's a great little secret!

What if you don't just have a cold, but really are sick? In more dire circumstances it would be wise to prepare someone ahead of time. If you want to power through but have an inkling you may need assistance, don't be a hero. Ask for help. I once had someone ask me to accompany them to a speech because they weren't sure how well they would hold up. That works too if you don't want to alert the organizer.

If you ever feel faint, get yourself to a seated position as fast as you can. This is not the time to worry about what everyone else is thinking about you. Passing out and hitting your head will make things worse.

If you know my story, you know I had 3 strokes in my late 30's. I wasn't in front of a room, but my point is that bad stuff can happen to anyone, at any age. Know your limits and know when to ask for help.

Fires and Other Natural Disasters

What if there's a fire alarm or other type of emergency alarm or announcement? You may not want to think about this, but when you accepted that speaking assignment, you also agreed to take ownership and leadership of the room for a short period of time. There may be someone else in the room that knows the facility better than you do, but often there isn't anyone else. Make it a practice to make a mental note of emergency exits when you first enter the building.

The reason why I even mention this is because I have actually read something quite different. I once read that if a fire or other emergency arises, a public speaker's duty is to continue to talk in a quiet and unassuming manner . . .

Wait, *WHAT!?!*

No, no, no! You are a not a musician on the Titanic! If an emergency alarm goes off, stop talking! Your priority just shifted to being a responsible leader and you need to assist in leading everyone out of the building or to shelter. Don't ever assume it's a false alarm unless you have been instructed by someone in authority at that facility.

Don't let me freak you out with all this talk of what could go wrong. The unexpected will happen, you will be unprepared at times and that's OK! Don't beat yourself up for apologizing for a cold or wishing you had a better comeback for that difficult audience member. Much of what I'm covering has taken me literally decades to learn and put into practice. Even ten years ago I couldn't think on my feet as well as I can now.

We're never going to be perfect. That's just part of the human experience, so give yourself room. Room to be fallible. To be human.

20

Next Steps

Are you ready to do more public speaking? Do you want to get better?

Go seek out opportunities.

Volunteer at the committee meeting to introduce the speaker at the next event, raise your hand when the teacher is seeking students to speak at an assembly, speak up at your board meeting. Find positions where you will have an opportunity to get in front of people.

Accept every opportunity to speak, no matter how small the crowd. Use every single event as practice.

Get involved in a group like Toastmasters where you'll have the opportunity to speak.

I do need to warn you of a phenomenon that might take place: The more experienced you become, the more you'll start to feel the fear and stress diminish in the time *leading up* to your speech, only to experience a spastic flurry of butterflies *while speaking*. This is normal!

You see, when we start doing something new it often heightens our fear because we're actually doing the thing that frightened us. It's our focus; we are now in the thick of the very thing we wanted to avoid in the first place! The good news is that the more you do that new thing, the more used to it you become. It becomes your new normal.

The more experienced you are in public speaking, the more you can convert that nervousness into positive, productive energy. This is the point at which you graduate from the tactical elements of public speaking to a focus on your state of being.

At first, this might seem counter to what you read earlier about getting the focus off of yourself. Not at all.

Once you have built your confidence and mastered the mechanics of public speaking, including those nerves, then you're ready to work on your mental state. Learning how to control your state is the highest level of public speaking mastery.

You've probably seen footage of Olympic athletes with their headphones on, looking like they're in a whole different world. Many of them use visualization techniques as they mentally run through their routine or their plays. They are getting themselves in a mental state to compete.

Think about how you can apply this to speaking. Is there music that really energizes you, inspires you and makes you feel like you can take on anything? Listen to that! Visualize yourself delivering your speech flawlessly and receiving a warm reception from the audience. Experiment with different things until you uncover what puts you in the absolute best, positive state to deliver a killer speech!

My secret? Because I have been using these warm-up exercises in this book for over twenty years, they get me in that peak mental state. Over time, they may do the same for you. I also use incantations, along with practicing my opening remarks and main points. All of these things keep me hyper–focused and energized.

Keep learning. Watch TED Talks, pay to hear well-known speakers. Observe their mannerisms, pacing, use of pauses and jokes. You can learn from these masters. Certainly, I have had years of critically evaluating speakers which gives me a bit of an edge, but once you start paying closer attention, you too will start picking up on things that can help you.

Avoiding embarrassment and humiliation in public speaking is easy enough when you devote yourself to preparation. I hope that you will find that you are so prepared for your next event that when you "sink to your level of preparation" it is a level you are proud of, a level to which you have worked hard to achieve, and a level that leaves your audience wanting more.

21

Warm Up Exercises

Warming up your vocal cords is something that's probably foreign to you unless you've been in the performing arts. Allow me to quickly explain.

A vocal warm-up is as crucial to an actor or singer's performance as the actual material he or she will perform. Just as you would warm up before a hard work out, you will want to warm up your vocal cords. It also goes deeper; by performing warm-up exercises you will engage your brain, your tongue, and your facial muscles. Your brain and mouth will start working together more effortlessly.

These are the same exercises you practiced earlier. Great for enunciation, breath control and warming up!

Exercise 1

Re**d** Leather, Yell**ow** Leather
Goo**d** Bloo**d**, Ba**d** Bloo**d**

Re**d** Leather, Yell**ow** Leather
Goo**d** Bloo**d**, Ba**d** Bloo**d**

Re**d** Leather, Yell**ow** Leather
Goo**d** Bloo**d**, Ba**d** Bloo**d**

Exercise 2

Wha**t to do to** die to**day**
A**t** a minu**t**e or two 'til **t**wo
A thing di**stinctly** har**d to** say
But har**d**er still **to do**
For they'll be a**t tattoo** at a twe**nty** 'til **t**wo
At a twe**nty** 'til **t**wo 'til two today
An**d** the dragon will come a**t** the bea**t** of the drum
A**t** a minu**t**e or two 'til **t**wo
A**t** a minu**t**e or two 'til **t**wo **to**day
A**t** a minu**t**e or two 'til **t**wo

Exercise 3

A tutor who tu**tored** the flute
Trie**d to** tu**to**r **t**wo tutors **t**o too**t**
Sai**d** the two **to** the tutor,
Is i**t** har**d**er **to** toot, or
To tutor two tutors **to** toot?

Exercise 4

I'm a mother pheasant **pl**ucker
I **pl**uck mother pheasants
I'm the most pleasant mother pheasant **pl**ucker
That ever **pl**ucke**d** a mother pheasant.

Exercise 5

One Hen

Two ducks

Three squawking geese

Four Limerick oysters

Five corpulent porpoises

Six pairs of Don Alvero's tweezers

Seven thousand Macedonians in full battle array

Eight brass monkeys from the ancient sacred crypts of Egypt

Nine apathetic, diabetic, sympathetic old men on roller skates who have a marked propensity towards procrastination and sloth

Ten lyrical, spherical, diabolical, denizens of the deep who all stalk around the crack in the corner of the quarry at the same time

Works Cited

1. http://www.tandfonline.com/doi/full/10.1080/08824096.2012.667772

2. "Nervous" *Dictionary.com*
3. "Excited"*Dictionary.com*

4. https://en.wikipedia.org/wiki/Announcer%27s_test

5. The National Center for Voice and Speech http://www.ncvs.org/ncvs/tutorials/voiceprod/tutorial/quality.html

6. "Fair Use": dictionary.com

7. "Prop": dictionary.com

8. "Edify": dictionary.com

Hire Leah

Comprehensive public speaking coaching requires a coach to hear and see the individual in action. Leah coaches individuals one-on-one and also provides group and corporate training.

For more information contact:

Tel: +1.888.723.7194
Leah@visionforcemarketing.com

Also by Leah Hoppes

Marketing Chomp: Powerful Modern Marketing to Grow Your Business Now

Take a bite out of the competition with marketing strategy. This will challenge the way you think about marketing, your message and your customers. Complete with exercises and a marketing plan template.

Available in print & audio: www.marketingchomp.com

About the Author

Leah Hoppes has over 30 years of public speaking experience, from competitive speech team, theatre, corporate presentations, training and workshops. She coaches speakers of all experience levels and helps them take control of their nerves, remove distracting habits and become more polished, engaging speakers.

Leah graduated from Valparaiso University and received her Marketing Certificate from University of Wisconsin – Madison. She is actively involved in her local Chamber of Commerce.

Leah and her husband, Sean Matthew Whitfield, are the co-founders of Vision Force Marketing. Vision Force Marketing provides strategic marketing planning, branding strategy, digital marketing, website design, logo design and more. Leah and Sean are frequent speakers and trainers on topics like public speaking, marketing, sales, entrepreneurship and leadership.

www.ingramcontent.com/pod-product-compliance
Lightning Source LLC
Chambersburg PA
CBHW020617300426
44113CB00007B/679